C++ Exercises with Data Structures and Algorithms

ISBN: 9798322690375

Table of Contents

1. University Courses

Let's create a program that will handle the enrollment for university courses. Each course has one or more prerequisites, i.e. courses that must have been completed by a student in order to be able to enroll in the specific one.

Proposed Solution

First of all, we will define the class for a student in the university:

```cpp
#include <iostream>
#include <string>

#define MAX_COURSES 100

using namespace std;

// Structure to represent a student
class Student
{
public:
  int id;
  string name;
  int courses[MAX_COURSES];
  int courseCount;
};
```

Listing 1-1: UniversityCourses.cpp

This class contains information about the student and the courses that have been completed successfully. The `courses` array contains the ID of the course.

Next, we define a class for the university courses:

```cpp
// Structure to represent a course
class Course
{
public:
  int id;
  string name;
  int prereqCount;
  int prereqIDs[MAX_COURSES]; // IDs of prerequisite courses

  // Check if a student can enroll in a course
  bool canEnroll(Student student)
  {
    for (int i = 0; i < prereqCount; ++i)
    {
      bool hasPrereq = false;
      for (int j = 0; j < student.courseCount; ++j)
      {
        if (student.courses[j] == prereqIDs[i])
        {
          hasPrereq = true;
```

```
            break;
        }
    }
    if (!hasPrereq)
    {
      return false;
    }
  }
  return true;
  }
};
```

Listing 1-2: UniversityCourses.cpp

Each course contains an array of the IDs of the prerequisite courses.

The class also includes a function that finds out whether a student can enroll at a course. For each prerequisite course, this function tries to match it with a course already taken by the student.

Finally, the main() function:

```
int main()
{
  // Sample course data
  Course courses[] = {
      {0, "Intro to Programming", 0, {-1}},// -1 represents no prerequisite
      {1, "Data Structures", 1, {0}},
      {2, "Algorithms", 1, {1}},
      {3, "Database Management", 1, {0}},
      {4, "Web Development", 1, {0}},
      {5, "Operating Systems", 2, {1, 2}},
      {6, "Computer Networks", 2, {1, 5}},
      {7, "Software Engineering", 2, {1, 2}},
      {8, "Machine Learning", 2, {1, 2}},
      {9, "Distributed Systems", 1, {5}},
      {10, "Cybersecurity", 2, {2, 3}},
      {11, "Cloud Computing", 2, {2, 3}},
      {12, "Mobile App Development", 1, {4}},
      {13, "Game Development", 1, {0}},
      {14, "Artificial Intelligence", 2, {2, 8}},
      {15, "Big Data Analytics", 2, {2, 3}},
      {16, "Blockchain Technology", 2, {2, 3}},
      {17, "UI/UX Design", 1, {14}},
      {18, "Embedded Systems", 2, {1, 5}},
      {19, "Computer Graphics", 1, {0}}
  };

  // Create a sample student
  Student student;
  student.id = 1;
  student.name = "John Doe";
  student.courseCount = 5;
  student.courses[0] = 0; // Intro to Programming
```

```
student.courses[1] = 1; // Data Structures
student.courses[2] = 2; // Algorithms
student.courses[3] = 3; // Database Management
student.courses[4] = 4; // Web Development

// Check if the student can enroll in specific courses
Course targetCourses[] = {
    courses[13], // Game Development
    courses[16], // Blockchain Technology
    courses[17], // UI/UX Design (student cannot enroll)
    courses[18]  // Embedded Systems
};

cout << "Enrollment status for " << student.name << ": " << endl;
for (int i = 0; i < 4; ++i)
{ // Loop through all four courses
  if (targetCourses[i].canEnroll(student))
  {
    cout << "- Can enroll in " << targetCourses[i].name << endl;
  }
  else
  {
    cout << "- Cannot enroll in " << targetCourses[i].name
         << " due to missing prerequisites." << endl;
  }
}

return 0;
}
```

Listing 1-3: UniversityCourses.cpp

We create sample courses and a sample user that is still at the earlier stages of studies. We then try to find out if this student can enroll at 4 specific courses. We will see that the student will not be able to enroll at the most advanced ones, for lack of successfully completed prerequisite courses.

You can find this project in GitHub:

https://github.com/htset/cpp_exercises_dsa/tree/master/UniversityCourses

2. Restaurant Reservations

For this exercise, we will create a small program that will create table reservations for a restaurant. Each table is characterized by its capacity. For simplicity, we will split the reservation time in one-hour slots; a reservation can span multiple consecutive slots.

Proposed Solution

First of all, we will define the class for a customer:

```cpp
#include <iostream>
#include <vector>
#include <algorithm>

using namespace std;

class Customer
{
public:
  Customer(string name) : name(name) {}

  string getName()
  {
    return name;
  }

private:
  string name;
};
```

Listing 2-1: Restaurant.cpp

This class contains the name of the customer. It could also include the customer phone number or other details.

Next, we define a class for the restaurant tables:

```cpp
class Table
{
public:
  Table(int id, int capacity) : id(id), capacity(capacity) {}

  int getCapacity()
  {
    return capacity;
  }

  int getID()
  {
    return id;
  }

private:
  int id;
```

```
  int capacity;
};
```

Listing 2-2: Restaurant.cpp

Each table object contains its ID as well as information about its capacity.

Next, we define the Reservation class:

```
class Reservation
{
public:
  Reservation(Customer* customer, Table* table,
    int startTimeSlot, int endTimeSlot)
    : customer(customer), table(table),
    startTimeSlot(startTimeSlot), endTimeSlot(endTimeSlot) {}

  Customer* getCustomer()
  {
    return customer;
  }

  Table* getTable()
  {
    return table;
  }

  int getStartTimeSlot()
  {
    return startTimeSlot;
  }

  int getEndTimeSlot()
  {
    return endTimeSlot;
  }
private:
  Customer* customer;
  Table* table;
  int startTimeSlot;
  int endTimeSlot;
};
```

Listing 2-3: Restaurant.cpp

Each reservation contains pointers to Customer and Table objects. It also contains the starting and the ending time slot (not inclusive).

We also create a Restaurant class that will implement the functionality for the creation of new reservations:

```
class Restaurant
{
```

```cpp
public:
  Restaurant() {}

  void addTable(Table* table)
  {
    tables.push_back(table);
  }

  // Find if table is available in specified timeslot
  bool isTableAvailable(Table* table, int startTimeSlot, int endTimeSlot)
  {
    for (Reservation* reservation : reservations)
    {
      if (reservation->getTable()->getID() == table->getID() &&
        ((startTimeSlot >= reservation->getStartTimeSlot()
          && startTimeSlot < reservation->getEndTimeSlot())
        ||
          (endTimeSlot > reservation->getStartTimeSlot()
            && endTimeSlot <= reservation->getEndTimeSlot())
        ||
          (startTimeSlot <= reservation->getStartTimeSlot()
            && endTimeSlot >= reservation->getEndTimeSlot())))
      {
        return false;
      }
    }
    return true;
  }

  // Find available tables for specified timeslots
  vector<Table*> findAvailableTables(int capacity, int startTimeSlot, int
endTimeSlot)
  {
    vector<Table*> availableTables;
    for (Table* table : tables)
    {
      if (table->getCapacity() >= capacity
        && isTableAvailable(table, startTimeSlot, endTimeSlot))
      {
        availableTables.push_back(table);
      }
    }
    // Sort available tables by capacity in ascending order
    sort(availableTables.begin(), availableTables.end(),
      [](Table* a, Table* b)
      { return a->getCapacity() < b->getCapacity(); });

    return availableTables;
  }

  void addReservation(const char* name, int capacity, int startSlot, int endSlot)
  {
    vector<Table*> availableTables = findAvailableTables(capacity,
                                                startSlot, endSlot);
```

```cpp
            if (!availableTables.empty())
            {
                // if a suitable table is found, create a reservation
                reservations.push_back(new Reservation(
                                            new Customer(name),
                                            availableTables.front(),
                                            startSlot,
                                            endSlot));
                cout << "Reservation successfully added.\n";
            }
            else
            {
                cout << "No available tables for the requested time slot.\n";
            }
        }

        void printReservations()
        {
            cout << "All reservations:\n";
            for (Reservation* reservation : reservations)
            {
                cout << "Customer: " << reservation->getCustomer()->getName()
                    << ", Table Capacity: " << reservation->getTable()->getCapacity()
                    << ", Start Time Slot: " << reservation->getStartTimeSlot()
                    << ", End Time Slot: " << reservation->getEndTimeSlot() << "\n";
            }
        }

private:
    vector<Table*> tables;
    vector<Reservation*> reservations;
};
```

Listing 2-4: Restaurant.cpp

Function `addTable()` adds the pointer of a table into the `tables` vector. Function `isTableAvailable()` determines whether a table is reserved or not, in the specified timeslot. To achieve this, we iterate in the `reservations` vector, and we check for this table's existing reservations.

Function `findAvailableTables()` searches this vector in order to find all the tables that are available inside the specified timeslot. The tables that are found, are then inserted into a new vector. This vector is returned after being sorted in ascending order, according to the table capacity.

Note how we provide the `sort()` function with a function that describes the type of comparison the `sort()` should perform on the objects. Here, we compare objects based on the `capacity` property.

Next, the addReservation() function will create a new reservation on the fly and will insert it (its pointer actually) into the reservations vector. That's of course, if a suitable table is found.

Finally, the main() function:

```cpp
int main()
{
  Restaurant restaurant;

  // Add tables
  restaurant.addTable(new Table(1,6));
  restaurant.addTable(new Table(2,4));
  restaurant.addTable(new Table(3,2));

  // Find available tables for a new reservation
  restaurant.addReservation("Customer 1", 4, 1, 3);
  restaurant.addReservation("Customer 2", 6, 2, 4);
  restaurant.addReservation("Customer 3", 4, 3, 5);
  restaurant.addReservation("Customer 4", 4, 1, 3);

  restaurant.printReservations();

  return 0;
}
```

Listing 2-5: Restaurant.cpp

We add tables to the Restaurant object and try to make reservations for specific capacities and timeslots. Some will be successful, but for others there will not be any table available. At the end, we print all the available reservations in the system.

You can find this project in GitHub:

https://github.com/htset/cpp_exercises_dsa/tree/master/Restaurant

3. Library

Here we will create a console application for a library. Users will be able to enter books and list all the titles available in the library. They will also be able to lend books, return books as well as list all the book lending events. The books and and the lending events will be stored in binary files.

Proposed Solution

Let's begin with the definition of the Book and LendingEvent structs:

```
#include <iostream>
#include <fstream>
#include <cstring>
#include <ctime>

struct Book
{
  char title[100];
  char author[100];
  int available;
};

struct LendingEvent
{
  char bookTitle[100];
  char userName[100];
  time_t lendingDate;
  int returned;
};
```

Listing 3-1: Library.cpp

For each book, we record the title and the author. We also keep information about whether it is available or is currently lent.

For each lending event we record the book title and the name of the library user that has borrowed it. We also keep the lending date as well as a boolean value of whether it has been returned or not.

We will use C-strings for the implementation of the structs. That's because we will store the book and lending event information into the binary file as whole objects. If we used string objects, then we would fail to store the actual data, as it is not stored inside the object but in the heap. As a result, we would end up storing pointers inside the binary files, which does not make much sense. When we close our program, the string object will be destroyed and the stored pointers will point to irrelevant positions in the memory.

We also define the Library class, that contains all the functionality for adding and displaying book information:

```
class Library
```

```cpp
{
public:
  void book_add();
  void book_list();
  void book_lend();
  void book_return();
  void lending_events_list();
private:
  const std::string booksFilename = "books.bin";
  const std::string lendingFilename = "lending_events.bin";
  void create_books_file(const std::string& filename);
  void create_lending_events_file(const std::string& filename);
};
```

Listing 3-2: Library.cpp

Let's implement the functionality to add a new book in library catalog:

```cpp
void Library::book_add()
{
  std::ofstream file(booksFilename, std::ios::binary | std::ios::app);
  if (!file.is_open())
  {
    create_books_file(booksFilename);
    file.open(booksFilename, std::ios::binary | std::ios::app);
  }

  Book book;
  std::cout << "Book title: ";
  std::cin.getline(book.title, sizeof(book.title));

  std::cout << "Author: ";
  std::cin.getline(book.author, sizeof(book.author));

  book.available = 1;

  file.seekp(0, std::ios::end);
  file.write(reinterpret_cast<const char*>(&book), sizeof(Book));
  file.close();
  std::cout << "Book added successfully.\n";
}
```

Listing 3-3: Library.cpp

At the beginning, we open the books file using ofstream as binary (std::ios::binary). We also specify that we will append data to the end (std::ios::app). If there is no file available (i.e., on the first time we run the program), then we move to create it (function create_books_file).

After we get the book title and author from the user, we proceed with moving to the end of the file and writing the new book object at this point:

```cpp
file.seekp(0, std::ios::end);
file.write(reinterpret_cast<const char*>(&book), sizeof(Book));
```

```
  file.close();
```

Function `seekp()` moves the file cursor at a distance of zero bytes from the end (`std::ios::end`) of the file. We use the `write()` function to write the whole object into the binary file; note that we pass the *address* of this object.

Next, we implement the listing of the books:

```
void Library::book_list()
{
  std::ifstream file(booksFilename, std::ios::binary | std::ios::app);
  if (!file.is_open())
  {
    create_books_file(booksFilename);
    file.open(booksFilename, std::ios::binary | std::ios::app);
  }

  Book book;
  std::cout << "Books available in the library:\n";
  while (file.read(reinterpret_cast<char*>(&book), sizeof(Book)))
  {
    std::cout << "Title: " << book.title << std::endl;
    std::cout << "Author: " << book.author << std::endl;
    std::cout << "Available: " << (book.available == 1 ? "True" : "False") <<
std::endl;
    std::cout << "------------------------------\n";
  }
  file.close();
}
```

Listing 3-4: Library.cpp

Here, we open the file from the beginning and we use `read()` to read each book object from the binary file.

We proceed with the book lending functionality:

```
void Library::book_lend()
{
  std::fstream booksFile(booksFilename, std::ios::binary | std::ios::app |
std::ios::in | std::ios::out);
  if (!booksFile.is_open())
  {
    create_books_file(booksFilename);
    booksFile.open(booksFilename, std::ios::binary | std::ios::app | std::ios::in |
std::ios::out);
  }

  std::fstream lendingFile(lendingFilename, std::ios::binary | std::ios::app |
std::ios::in | std::ios::out);
  if (!lendingFile.is_open())
  {
    create_lending_events_file(lendingFilename);
```

```cpp
        lendingFile.open(lendingFilename, std::ios::binary | std::ios::app | std::ios::in
 | std::ios::out);
    }

    char bookTitle[100];
    char userName[100];
    std::cout << "Enter the title of the book to lend: ";
    std::cin.getline(bookTitle, sizeof(bookTitle));

    booksFile.seekg(0, std::ios::beg);
    std::cout << booksFile.tellg();

    Book book;
    int bookFound = 0;
    while (booksFile.read(reinterpret_cast<char*>(&book), sizeof(Book)))
    {
      if (strcmp(book.title, bookTitle) == 0 && book.available)
      {
        book.available = 0;
        booksFile.seekp(-static_cast<long>(sizeof(Book)), std::ios::cur);
        booksFile.write(reinterpret_cast<const char*>(&book), sizeof(Book));
        bookFound = 1;

        std::cout << "Enter your name: ";
        std::cin.getline(userName, sizeof(userName));

        LendingEvent event;
        strcpy(event.bookTitle, bookTitle);
        strcpy(event.userName, userName);
        event.lendingDate = time(nullptr);
        event.returned = 0;

        lendingFile.seekp(0, std::ios::end);
        lendingFile.write(reinterpret_cast<const char*>(&event), sizeof(LendingEvent));
        std::cout << "Book '" << bookTitle << "' has been lent to " << userName <<
".\n";
        break;
      }
    }
    if (!bookFound)
    {
      std::cout << "Book '" << bookTitle << "' not found or not available.\n";
    }

    booksFile.close();
    lendingFile.close();
}
```

Listing 3-5: Library.cpp

We first try to find the requested book by reading through the books file. When we find the
book (and if it is available), we mark it as not available and we write the book back to the

file. To perform this, we move the file cursor back by `sizeof(Book)` bytes (that's why we use a negative offset value):

```cpp
booksFile.seekp(-static_cast<long>(sizeof(Book)), std::ios::cur);
```

In this way, we go back to the beginning of the specific entry in the file, and we overwrite it:

```cpp
booksFile.write(reinterpret_cast<const char*>(&book), sizeof(Book));
```

Afterwards, we record the lending event by writing a new entry at the end of the respective binary file.

Next, we present the functionality for returning a book:

```cpp
void Library::book_return()
{
  std::fstream booksFile(booksFilename, std::ios::binary | std::ios::app |
std::ios::in | std::ios::out);
  if (!booksFile.is_open())
    {
      create_books_file(booksFilename);
      booksFile.open(booksFilename, std::ios::binary | std::ios::app | std::ios::in |
std::ios::out);
    }

  std::fstream lendingFile(lendingFilename, std::ios::binary | std::ios::app |
std::ios::in | std::ios::out);
  if (!lendingFile.is_open())
    {
      create_lending_events_file(lendingFilename);
      lendingFile.open(lendingFilename, std::ios::binary | std::ios::app | std::ios::in
| std::ios::out);
    }

  char bookTitle[100];
  std::cout << "Enter the title of the book to return: ";
  std::cin.getline(bookTitle, sizeof(bookTitle));

  booksFile.seekg(0, std::ios::beg);

  Book book;
  int bookFound = 0;
  while (booksFile.read(reinterpret_cast<char*>(&book), sizeof(Book)))
    {
      if (strcmp(book.title, bookTitle) == 0 && !book.available)
        {
          book.available = 1;
          booksFile.seekp(-static_cast<long>(sizeof(Book)), std::ios::cur);
          booksFile.write(reinterpret_cast<const char*>(&book), sizeof(Book));
          bookFound = 1;

          lendingFile.seekg(0, std::ios::beg);
```

```
        LendingEvent event;
        while (lendingFile.read(reinterpret_cast<char*>(&event), sizeof(LendingEvent)))
        {
          if (strcmp(event.bookTitle, bookTitle) == 0 && !event.returned)
          {
            event.returned = 1;
            lendingFile.seekp(-static_cast<long>(sizeof(LendingEvent)), std::ios::cur);
            lendingFile.write(reinterpret_cast<const char*>(&event),
              sizeof(LendingEvent));
            std::cout << "Book '" << bookTitle << "' has been returned.\n";
            break;
          }
        }
        break;
      }
    }
    if (!bookFound)
    {
      std::cout << "Book '" << bookTitle << "' not found or already returned.\n";
    }

    booksFile.close();
    lendingFile.close();
}
```

Listing 3-6: Library.cpp

Here, we search in the lending events file for a lending event about the specific book and we modify the entry by setting the returned variable to 1.

Now, let's see the events listing function:

```
void Library::lending_events_list()
{
  std::ifstream lendingFile(lendingFilename, std::ios::binary);
  if (!lendingFile.is_open())
  {
    create_lending_events_file(lendingFilename);
    lendingFile.open(lendingFilename, std::ios::binary);
  }

  LendingEvent event;
  std::cout << "Lending events:\n";
  while (lendingFile.read(reinterpret_cast<char*>(&event), sizeof(LendingEvent)))
  {
    std::cout << "Book Title: " << event.bookTitle << std::endl;
    std::cout << "User Name: " << event.userName << std::endl;
    std::cout << "Lending Date: " << ctime(&event.lendingDate);
    std::cout << "Returned: " << (event.returned == 1 ? "True" : "False") <<
std::endl;
    std::cout << "----------------------------\n";
    std::cout << std::endl;
  }
}
```

Listing 3-7: Library.cpp

Next, we present the *private* functions that create the two files:

```cpp
void Library::create_books_file(const std::string& filename)
{
  std::ofstream file(filename, std::ios::binary | std::ios::app);
  if (!file.is_open())
  {
    std::cerr << "Error creating books file.\n";
    exit(1);
  }
  std::cout << "Books file created successfully.\n";
}

void Library::create_lending_events_file(const std::string& filename)
{
  std::ofstream file(filename, std::ios::binary | std::ios::app);
  if (!file.is_open())
  {
    std::cerr << "Error creating lending events file.\n";
    exit(1);
  }
  std::cout << "Lending events file created successfully.\n";
}
```

Listing 3-8: Library.cpp

And finally, the main() function that handles the interaction with the user:

```cpp
int main()
{
  Library lib;
  int choice;
  do
  {
    std::cout << "\n1. Add a book\n2. List all books\n3. Lend a book\n4. Return a
book\n5. List lending events\n0. Exit\n";
    std::cout << "Enter your choice: ";
    std::cin >> choice;
    std::cin.ignore(); // Consume newline left in the buffer by cin

    switch (choice)
    {
    case 1:
      lib.book_add();
      break;
    case 2:
      lib.book_list();
      break;
    case 3:
      lib.book_lend();
      break;
    case 4:
```

```cpp
      lib.book_return();
      break;
    case 5:
      lib.lending_events_list();
      break;
    case 0:
      std::cout << "Exiting.\n";
      break;
    default:
      std::cout << "Invalid choice. Please try again.\n";
    }

  } while (choice != 0);

  return 0;
}
```

Listing 3-9: Library.cpp

You can find this project in GitHub:

https://github.com/htset/cpp_exercises_dsa/tree/master/Library

4. Contact List

In this exercise, we will create a list that will store the names and the phone numbers of our contacts. For faster search performance, the contacts will be stored in a *hash map* structure.

Proposed Solution

A *hash map*, also known as a *hash table*, is a data structure that efficiently organizes and retrieves data based on key-value pairs. It employs a technique called *hashing*, where each key is mapped to a unique index in an array using a hash function. This mapping allows for rapid insertion, deletion, and retrieval of values based on their associated keys.

In cases where multiple keys hash to the same index (known as *collisions*), hash maps often employ strategies such as *chaining* to handle these collisions gracefully and maintain performance.

Here is the definition of the classes used:

```cpp
#include <iostream>
#define HASH_SIZE 100

using namespace std;

class Contact
{
public:
   string name;
   string phone;
   Contact* next;
};

class ContactList
{
public:
   Contact* bucket_table[HASH_SIZE];

   ContactList();
   unsigned int hash(const char* name);
   void contact_add(string name, string phone);
   void contact_remove(string name);
   void contact_search(string name);
};
```

Listing 4-1: ContactList.cpp

The ContactList class contains a table of 100 entries. Each entry contains a pointer to a Contact object. The Contact class contains the name and the phone number, as well as a pointer to another Contact object, making it a linked list node. Essentially, the ContactList class is an array of linked lists; in this way the contact list can expand as we add new elements, avoiding collisions.

A contact will be instered into one of the buckets according to its specific hash number. We will use a hash function that will create a number between 0 and 99 based on the contact's name string:

```cpp
unsigned int ContactList::hash(const char* name)
{
  unsigned int hash = 0;
  int c;
  while (c = *name++)
  {
    hash = ((hash << 5) + hash) + c;
  }
  return hash % HASH_SIZE;
}
```

Listing 4-2: ContactList.cpp

This function is based on a hash function written by Daniel J. Bernstein (also know as *djb*)[1]. This function returns the index of the hash map, where we should insert the specific contact.

In the class constructor we initialize the buckets with nulls:

```cpp
ContactList::ContactList()
{
  for (int i = 0; i < HASH_SIZE; i++)
  {
    bucket_table[i] = nullptr;
  }
}
```

Listing 4-3: ContactList.cpp

Here is the code for the contact addition:

```cpp
void ContactList::contact_add(string name, string phone)
{
  unsigned int hash_index = hash(name.c_str());
  Contact* new_contact = new Contact();
  if (!new_contact)
  {
    cout << "Memory allocation failed." << endl;
    return;
  }
  new_contact->name = name;
  new_contact->phone = phone;
  new_contact->next = this->bucket_table[hash_index];
  this->bucket_table[hash_index] = new_contact;
}
```

Listing 4-4: ContactList.cpp

---

[1] http://www.cse.yorku.ca/~oz/hash.html

We first calculate the hash index based on the contact's name. Note the use of string's c_str() function that gives us the underlying C-string. Then we create a new Contact object. After populating the object variables, we insert the object at the beginning of the respective bucket.

Here is the code for contact removal:

```cpp
void ContactList::contact_remove(string name)
{
  unsigned int index = hash(name.c_str());
  Contact* contact = this->bucket_table[index];
  Contact* previous = nullptr;

  while (contact != nullptr)
  {
    if (contact->name == name)
    {
      if (previous == nullptr)
      {
        // Contact to remove is the head of the list
        this->bucket_table[index] = contact->next;
      }
      else
      {
        // Contact to remove is not the head of the list
        previous->next = contact->next;
      }
      delete contact;
      cout << "Contact '" << name << "' removed successfully." << endl;
      return;
    }
    previous = contact;
    contact = contact->next;
  }
  cout << "Contact '" << name << "' not found." << endl;
}
```

Listing 4-5: ContactList.cpp

To remove an entry, we first need to get its hash value. We use this integer value as the index to get the respective bucket. We then search the bucket entries, one by one, until we locate the specific contact. We then remove the entry from the buckets, in the same way we remove a node from a linked list.

Next, the code for contact search is presented:

```cpp
void ContactList::contact_search(string name)
{
  unsigned int hash_index = hash(name.c_str());
  Contact* contact = this->bucket_table[hash_index];
  while (contact != nullptr)
  {
    if (contact->name == name)
```

```
    {
      cout << "Name: " << contact->name
           << "\nPhone Number : " << contact->phone << endl;
      return;
    }
    contact = contact->next;
  }
  cout << "Contact '" << name << "' not found." << endl;
}
```

Finally, in the main() function, we create a phonebook and we use it to add, remove and search contacts:

```
int main()
{
  ContactList phonebook;
  phonebook.contact_add("John", "235454545");
  phonebook.contact_add("Jane", "775755454");
  phonebook.contact_add("George", "4344343477");

  phonebook.contact_search("John");
  phonebook.contact_search("Alex");
  phonebook.contact_search("George");

  phonebook.contact_remove("Jake");
  phonebook.contact_remove("Jane");
  phonebook.contact_search("Jane");

  return 0;
}
```

You can find this project in GitHub:

https://github.com/htset/cpp_exercises_dsa/tree/master/ContactList

5. Priority Todo List

We are going to implement a simple todo list application. Each entry will contain the task description as well as a number that will signify its priority (top priority is equal to 1).

The todo list will be implemented using a *linked list*. Apart from the options to add, delete and display tasks, there will also be functionality to sort the linked list using *bubble sort*.

Proposed Solution

Let's start with the definition of the linked list structure:

```cpp
#include <iostream>
#include <string>
using namespace std;

class Task
{
public:
  string description;
  int priority;
  Task* next;
};

class TodoList
{
  Task* head;
  int size;

public:
  TodoList();
  void add_task(string description, int priority);
  void remove_task(int index);
  void display_tasks();
  void sort_tasks();
};
```

Listing 5-1: Todo.cpp

The linked list consists of Task nodes that get linked one to the other via the next pointer. The head variable points to the first element in the list.

First let's see the main() function:

```cpp
int main()
{
  TodoList list;

  int choice;
  string description;
  int priority;
  int index;
```

```cpp
    do
    {
        cout << "\nTo-Do List Manager" << endl;
        cout << "1. Add Task" << endl;
        cout << "2. Remove Task" << endl;
        cout << "3. Display Tasks" << endl;
        cout << "4. Sort Tasks by Priority" << endl;
        cout << "0. Exit" << endl;
        cout << "Enter your choice: ";
        cin >> choice;
        cin.ignore();

        switch (choice)
        {
        case 1:
            cout << "Enter task description: ";
            getline(cin, description);
            cout << "Enter priority: ";
            cin >> priority;
            cin.ignore();
            list.add_task(description, priority);
            cout << "Task added successfully." << endl;
            break;
        case 2:
            cout << "Enter number of task to remove: ";
            cin >> index;
            cin.ignore();
            list.remove_task(index - 1);
            cout << "Task removed successfully." << endl;
            break;
        case 3:
            cout << "List of tasks:" << endl;
            list.display_tasks();
            break;
        case 4:
            list.sort_tasks();
            cout << "Tasks sorted by priority." << endl;
            break;
        case 5:
            cout << "Exiting..." << endl;
            break;
        default:
            cout << "Invalid choice. Please try again." << endl;
        }
    } while (choice != 0);

    return 0;
}
```

Listing 5-2: Todo.cpp

The main function handles the user input and calls the respective functions of the todo list. Note the use of the `cin.ignore()` function. It is used immediately after the >> input operator, in order to remove the newline character from the input stream. If we fail to use it, then the next input operation (either with >> or with `getline`) will consume this newline and will stop there, without taking actual input.

The class constructor initializes the linked list structure:

```cpp
TodoList::TodoList()
{
  this->head = nullptr;
  this->size = 0;
}
```

Listing 5-3: Todo.cpp

The `add_task()` function allocates memory for a new task node and inserts it at the end of the linked list:

```cpp
void TodoList::add_task(string description, int priority)
{
  Task* task = new Task;
  if (!task)
  {
    cout << "Memory allocation failed." << endl;
    return;
  }
  task->description = description;
  task->priority = priority;
  task->next = nullptr;

  if (this->head == nullptr)
  {
    // List is empty
    this->head = task;
  }
  else
  {
    Task* temp = this->head;
    // Find the last node
    while (temp->next != nullptr)
    {
      temp = temp->next;
    }
    // Insert the new task after the last node
    temp->next = task;
  }
  this->size++;
}
```

Listing 5-4: Todo.cpp

Next, we define the `remove_task()` function:

```cpp
void TodoList::remove_task(int index)
{
  if (this->head == nullptr)
```

```
{
  cout << "List is empty." << endl;
  return;
}

if (index == 0)
{
  // If we remove the first item in the list
  Task* temp = this->head;
  this->head = this->head->next;
  delete temp;
  this->size--;
  return;
}

Task* previous = nullptr;
Task* current = this->head;
int i = 0;
// Go to the selected index
while (current != nullptr && i < index)
{
  previous = current;
  current = current->next;
  i++;
}

if (current == nullptr)
{
  cout << "Index out of bounds." << endl;
  return;
}

previous->next = current->next;
delete current;
this->size--;
}
```

Listing 5-5: Todo.cpp

The argument to the function is the index of the entry inside the linked list, as it is presented during task listing. As we will see in the next snippet, we start listing the tasks from number 1, which is something that we take into account in the calculations above.

Here is the code for the task listing:

```
void TodoList::display_tasks()
{
  Task* temp = this->head;
  int i = 1;
  while (temp != nullptr)
  {
    cout << i++
      << ") Description: " << temp->description
      << ", Priority : " << temp->priority << endl;
```

```
    temp = temp->next;
  }
}
```

Listing 5-6: Todo.cpp

Finally, we present the code for the sorting of tasks according to their priority:

```
void TodoList::sort_tasks()
{
  int swapped;
  Task* ptr1;
  Task* ptr2 = nullptr;

  if (this->head == nullptr)
    return;

  do
  {
    swapped = 0; // will change if swapping happens
    ptr1 = this->head;

    while (ptr1->next != ptr2)
    {
      if (ptr1->priority > ptr1->next->priority)
      {
        // Swap data of adjacent nodes
        int tempPriority = ptr1->priority;
        ptr1->priority = ptr1->next->priority;
        ptr1->next->priority = tempPriority;

        string tempDescription;
        tempDescription = ptr1->description;
        ptr1->description = ptr1->next->description;
        ptr1->next->description = tempDescription;

        swapped = 1; // swap happened in this loop pass; don't stop yet
      }
      ptr1 = ptr1->next;
    }
    ptr2 = ptr1;
  } while (swapped); // quit loop when no swap happened
}
```

Listing 5-7: Todo.cpp

The code employs the *bubble sort* algorithm to perform the task sorting operation. In bubble sort, we perform multiple passes of the linked list. Each time we find a task that has lower priority than its next task, then we perform swapping of those adjacent tasks. Over time, all entries will be sorted according to priority and there will eventually be a loop pass where no swapping will occur. This is when the algorithm will end.

You can find this project in GitHub:

https://github.com/htset/cpp_exercises_dsa/tree/master/Todo

6. Songs List

Let's create a simple program that takes an array of songs and sorts them by artist, album or release date, using *insertion sort*.

Proposed Solution

The Song class will contain information about the title of the song, the artist, the album and the release year:

```cpp
#include <iostream>
#include <string>
using namespace std;

class Song
{
public:
  string title;
  string artist;
  string album;
  int release_year;
};
```

Listing 6-1: Songs.cpp

Next, we define three functions, that will be used for the comparisons:

```cpp
// Compare songs based on artist
int compareByArtist(const Song* a, const Song* b)
{
  return a->artist.compare(b->artist);
}

// Compare songs based on album
int compareByAlbum(const Song* a, const Song* b)
{
  return a->album.compare(b->album);
}

// Compare songs based on release date
int compareByReleaseDate(const Song* a, const Song* b)
{
  return a->release_year - b->release_year;
}
```

Listing 6-2: Songs.cpp

In the first two functions, we compare two strings, while in the third one we compare two integers. Those functions will be used by the insertionSort() function:

```cpp
void insertionSort(Song arr[], int n, int (*compare)(const Song*, const Song*))
{
  int i, j;
  Song key;
```

```
for (i = 1; i < n; i++)
{
   key = arr[i];
   j = i - 1;

   // Move elements of arr[0..i-1], that are greater than key,
   // to one position ahead of their current position
   while (j >= 0 && compare(&arr[j], &key) > 0)
   {
      arr[j + 1] = arr[j];
      j = j - 1;
   }
   arr[j + 1] = key;
}
}
```

Listing 6-3: Songs.cpp

First of all, we should note that we pass a function pointer (compare) as argument to insertionSort(). Function pointers in C++ contain the address of a function and can be used to create a callback mechanism. More specifically, when insertSort() calls compare(), it essentially calls the function whose pointer was passed when insertSort() was called.

For instance, if we call insertionSort() like this:

```
insertionSort(songs, num_songs, compareByArtist);
```

then, the following code inside insertionSort():

```
while (j >= 0 && compare(&arr[j], &key) > 0)
```

will result in calling the compareByArtist() function. In this way, we don't have to write insertionSort() three times to accommodate for the three different types of comparison.

Insertion sort works by taking each element in the array and moving it to the left part of the array in a sorted position. At any time, the left part of the array is sorted, while we take items from the right part. As we move an element to a place in the array, all the items to the right will have to move one place to the right.

This is all illustrated in the main() function where we call insertionSort() three times, each time passing a different comparison function. Each time, the array is sorted in a different way:

```
int main()
{
   Song songs[] = {
       {"Song1", "Artist2", "Album1", 2010},
       {"Song2", "Artist1", "Album2", 2005},
       {"Song3", "Artist3", "Album1", 2015},
       {"Song4", "Artist4", "Album3", 2008},
```

```cpp
    {"Song5", "Artist1", "Album2", 2003},
    {"Song6", "Artist3", "Album4", 2019},
    {"Song7", "Artist2", "Album3", 2012},
    {"Song8", "Artist4", "Album4", 2017},
    {"Song9", "Artist5", "Album5", 2014},
    {"Song10", "Artist5", "Album5", 2011} };

  int num_songs = sizeof(songs) / sizeof(songs[0]);

  // Sort by artist
  insertionSort(songs, num_songs, compareByArtist);
  cout << "Sorted by Artist:" << endl;
  for (int i = 0; i < num_songs; i++)
  {
    cout << songs[i].title << " from " << songs[i].artist << endl;
  }
  cout << endl;

  // Sort by album
  insertionSort(songs, num_songs, compareByAlbum);
  cout << "Sorted by Album:" << endl;
  for (int i = 0; i < num_songs; i++)
  {
    cout << songs[i].title << " from " << songs[i].album << endl;
  }
  cout << endl;

  // Sort by release date
  insertionSort(songs, num_songs, compareByReleaseDate);
  cout << "Sorted by Release Date:" << endl;
  for (int i = 0; i < num_songs; i++)
  {
    cout << songs[i].title << " released in " << songs[i].release_year << endl;
  }

  return 0;
}
```

Listing 6-4: Songs.cpp

You can find this project in GitHub:

https://github.com/htset/cpp_exercises_dsa/tree/master/Songs

7. Task allocation

We will create a program where users can enter the description of tasks and their durations. The tasks will be allocated to workers, based on the amount of work that they already have taken over. This means that the task will be allocated to the worker with the lower workload.

Proposed Solution

We will use a priority queue to express the differences in priority between the various workers, based on their workload so far.

Let's first define the Task and Worker classes:

```cpp
#include <iostream>
#include <queue>
#include <vector>
#include <string>

using namespace std;

// Task structure
class Task
{
public:
  string description;
  int duration;

  Task(const string& description, int duration)
    : description(description), duration(duration) {}
};

// Worker structure
class Worker
{
public:
  int id;
  int workload;

  Worker(int id, int workload)
    : id(id), workload(workload) {}

  // Overload the < operator for priority comparison
  bool operator<(const Worker& other) const
  {
    // Workers with shorter workload have higher priority
    return workload > other.workload;
  }
};
```

Listing 7-1: TaskAllocation.cpp

The Task class consists of the task description and duration in minutes. The Worker class contains the id of the worker as well as the workload, also in minutes.

Note the overloaded operator < that will be used for the comparison between workers based on the amount of workload they have been assigned.

Next, we define the main() function:

```cpp
void addTask(priority_queue<Worker>& workerQueue, vector<Task>& tasks);
void displayTasks(const vector<Task>& tasks);
void printWorkersQueue(const priority_queue<Worker>& workerQueue);

int main()
{
  vector<Task> tasks;
  priority_queue<Worker> workerQueue;

  int numWorkers;
  cout << "Enter the number of workers: ";
  cin >> numWorkers;
  cin.ignore();

  // Initialize workers with ID and 0 workload
  for (int i = 0; i < numWorkers; ++i)
  {
    workerQueue.push(Worker(i, 0));
  }

  int choice;
  do
  {
    cout << "\nMenu:\n1. Add Task\n2. Display Tasks\n3. Print Workers Queue\n4. Exit\nEnter your choice: ";
    cin >> choice;
    cin.ignore();

    switch (choice)
    {
    case 1:
      addTask(workerQueue, tasks);
      break;
    case 2:
      displayTasks(tasks);
      break;
    case 3:
      printWorkersQueue(workerQueue);
      break;
    case 4:
      cout << "Exiting program...\n";
      break;
    default:
      cout << "Invalid choice! Please try again.\n";
    }
  } while (choice != 4);
```

```
      return 0;
}
```

Listing 7-2: TaskAllocation.cpp

The `main()` function displays the menu and gets the user's selections. It also initializes a vector that will store the tasks, and a priority queue that will contain the workers.

When the program starts, we get to select the total number of workers; they will be referred to by their ID.

Next, we implement the function that adds a new task to the system:

```
// Function to add a task and allocate it to a worker
void addTask(priority_queue<Worker>& workerQueue, vector<Task>& tasks)
{
  string description;
  int duration;

  cout << "Enter task description: ";
  getline(cin, description);
  cout << "Enter task duration (in minutes): ";
  cin >> duration;
  cin.ignore();

  if (workerQueue.empty())
  {
    cout << "No workers available! Task cannot be assigned." << endl;
    return;
  }

  // Dequeue the worker with the shortest workload
  Worker worker = workerQueue.top();
  workerQueue.pop();

  // Assign the task to the worker and update workload
  tasks.push_back(Task(description, duration));
  cout << "Task added successfully and allocated to Worker "
    << worker.id << "!" << endl;

  // Update workload
  worker.workload += duration;
  // Enqueue the worker back with updated workload
  workerQueue.push(worker);
}
```

Listing 7-3: TaskAllocation.cpp

In order to find the worker that has the lowest workload, we store workers them in the priority queue. When we push the worker in the queue, then the `operator<` function from the `Worker` class is called in order to determine the position that the worker object will be inserted in the queue. The operator is used to compare the worker object with the other objects in the queue, based on their workload.

We get the worker with the lowest payload (the one that is positioned at the front of the queue) and we add the task's workload to the worker's own workload. Then we store the task into the tasks vector, after assigning the worker to the task. Finally, the worker is inserted into the queue again; now the worker will be positioned according to the newly updated workload.

Finally, we present the code for two other operations, displaying the tasks and the workers information respectively:

```cpp
// Function to display all tasks
void displayTasks(const vector<Task>& tasks)
{
  cout << "Task List:" << endl;
  for (const Task& task : tasks)
  {
    cout << "Task description: " << task.description
      << ", Duration: " << task.duration << " minutes" << endl;
  }
}


// Function to print the workers queue
void printWorkersQueue(const priority_queue<Worker>& workerQueue)
{
  priority_queue<Worker> tempQueue = workerQueue; // Create a copy of the queue
  cout << "Workers Queue:" << endl;
  while (!tempQueue.empty())
  {
    Worker worker = tempQueue.top();
    cout << "Worker ID: " << worker.id << ", Workload: "
      << worker.workload << " minutes" << endl;
    tempQueue.pop();
  }
}
```

Listing 7-4: TaskAllocation.cpp

To print the workers, we get a copy of the queue. We print each worker by popping each object from the new queue.

You can find this project in GitHub:

https://github.com/htset/cpp_exercises_dsa/tree/master/TaskAllocation

8. Word Frequencies

We will create a simple program that will parse a text file and will find the frequencies of all the words that appear in it.

Proposed Solution

This project is a use case for a map/dictionary structure. We will use a map class that will store word and word frequency pairs.

Here is the main function:

```cpp
#include <iostream>
#include <fstream>
#include <map>
#include <string>
#include <algorithm>
#include <cctype>

using namespace std;

string cleanWord(const string& word);

int main()
{
  map<string, int> wordFrequency;

  // Read text from file
  ifstream inputFile("input.txt");
  if (!inputFile)
  {
    cerr << "Error opening file." << endl;
    return 1;
  }

  // Process each word in the input
  string word;
  while (inputFile >> word)
  {
    word = cleanWord(word);
    if (!word.empty())
    {
      wordFrequency[word]++;
    }
  }

  inputFile.close();

  // Display word frequencies
  cout << "Word Frequencies:" << endl;
  for (const auto& pair : wordFrequency)
  {
    cout << pair.first << ": " << pair.second << endl;
  }
```

```
    return 0;
}
```

Listing 8-1: WordFrequency.cpp

By using `istream`'s `>>` operator, we are reading the input file, word by word. After processing each word, we use the following expression:

```
wordFrequency[word]++;
```

Two things may happen here:

- If the key does not already exist in the dictionary, then the key is inserted into the map. Since the map values are of integer type, the value is initialized to zero. The zero value then is increased to 1.
- If the key already exists in the dictionary, then the existing value is increased.

Finally, we employ a *for loop* to print all the words and their frequencies to the console.

Here is the word processing function:

```
// Clean and normalize a word
string cleanWord(const string& word)
{
  string cleanedWord;
  for (char c : word)
  {
    if (isalpha(c))
    {
      cleanedWord += tolower(c);
    }
  }
  return cleanedWord;
}
```

Listing 8-2: WordFrequency.cpp

We remove special characters, like parentheses etc., and we create a clean word where all letters are in lowercase.

You can find this project in GitHub:

https://github.com/htset/cpp_exercises_dsa/tree/master/WordFrequency

9. Syntax Checker

Let's create a trivial syntax checker that will scan a source code file and will determine whether the parentheses, brackets, or braces in the code are balanced or not.

Proposed Solution

In source code, when we open a series of parentheses, brackets, or braces, we have to make sure that they are closed in the reverse order.

The fact that items entered in a *stack* are extracted in the reverse order, makes it suitable for this algorithm:

```cpp
#include <iostream>
#include <string>
#include <fstream>
#define MAX_SIZE 100

using namespace std;

class Stack
{
  char items[MAX_SIZE];
  int top;

public:
  Stack();
  void push(char c);
  char pop();
  bool check_empty();
};
```

Listing 9-1: SyntaxChecker.cpp

Here is the code for the stack initialization:

```cpp
Stack::Stack()
{
  top = -1;
}
```

Listing 9-2: SyntaxChecker.cpp

Next, we add the code for stack *push* and *pop*, as well as a function to check if the stack is empty:

```cpp
void Stack::push(char c)
{
  if (top == MAX_SIZE - 1)
  {
    cout << "Stack is full" << endl;
    exit(1);
  }
```

```cpp
    items[++top] = c;
}

char Stack::pop()
{
  if (top == -1)
  {
    cout << "Stack is empty" << endl;
    exit(1);
  }
  return items[top--];
}

bool Stack::check_empty()
{
  return (top == -1);
}
```

Listing 9-3: SyntaxChecker.cpp

The most interesting part of the code is the algorithm that checks whether the file is balanced or not:

```cpp
int check_balanced(string filename)
{
  ifstream file(filename);
  if (!file.is_open())
  {
    cout << "Error opening file." << endl;
    exit(1);
  }

  char c;
  Stack stack;

  while (file.get(c))
  {
    if (c == '(' || c == '[' || c == '{')
    {
      stack.push(c);
    }
    else if (c == ')' || c == ']' || c == '}')
    {
      // If stack is empty --> Return 'Unbalanced'
      if (stack.check_empty())
      {
        file.close();
        return 0;
      }
      char openingChar = stack.pop();
      if ((c == ')' && openingChar != '(') ||
        (c == ']' && openingChar != '[') ||
        (c == '}' && openingChar != '{'))
      {
```

```
        file.close();
        // If closing character doesn't match top of stack
        // --> return 'Unbalanced'
        return 0;
      }
    }
  }

  // If stack is empty, after we have finished
  // checking the input file
  // --> return 'Balanced'
  int result = stack.check_empty();
  file.close();
  return result;
}
```

We open and parse the source code file, and we push the bracket *opening* characters into the stack. When we encounter a *closing* character, then we pop the first available opening character from the stack.

If there is a mismatch between those two characters, we conclude that the file is not balanced. At the end, we also check that the stack is emptied; if not, then the file is still unbalanced.

Note that this is a trivial version of the algorithm. In fact, if we try to check the exercises's own source file (*SytnaxChecker.cpp*) for parentheses balancing, we will get an error – even though the code compiles. That's because we use single characters (opening or closing) in our code during checking, like in the following line:

```
if (c == '(' || c == '[' || c == '{')
```

A more advanced version of the algorithm would not take those characters (e.g. those enclosed in quotes) into account.

You can find this project in GitHub:

https://github.com/htset/cpp_exercises_dsa/tree/master/SyntaxChecker

10. Maze Solver

In this exercise, we will use a *stack* to find our way through a maze.

Proposed Solution

We will define a maze as a two-dimensional array of integers. The walls will be marked with ones (1), while the corridors of the maze will be marked with zeroes (0).

Below, we can see the definition of a 15x15 maze:

```
int matrix[ROWS][COLS] = {
  {0, 1, 0, 0, 0, 0, 0, 0, 0, 0, 0, 0, 0, 0, 0},
  {0, 1, 0, 1, 0, 1, 1, 1, 1, 0, 1, 1, 1, 1, 0},
  {0, 1, 0, 1, 0, 1, 0, 0, 0, 0, 1, 0, 0, 0, 0},
  {0, 0, 0, 1, 0, 1, 0, 1, 1, 1, 1, 0, 1, 1, 0},
  {0, 1, 0, 1, 0, 1, 0, 0, 0, 0, 1, 0, 1, 0, 0},
  {0, 1, 0, 1, 0, 1, 1, 1, 1, 0, 1, 0, 1, 1, 0},
  {0, 1, 0, 1, 0, 0, 0, 0, 1, 0, 1, 0, 0, 0, 0},
  {0, 1, 0, 1, 1, 1, 1, 0, 1, 0, 1, 0, 1, 1, 0},
  {0, 1, 0, 0, 0, 0, 1, 0, 1, 0, 1, 0, 0, 1, 0},
  {0, 1, 1, 1, 1, 0, 1, 0, 1, 0, 1, 0, 1, 1, 0},
  {0, 0, 0, 0, 1, 0, 1, 0, 1, 0, 1, 0, 0, 0, 0},
  {0, 1, 1, 0, 1, 0, 1, 0, 1, 0, 1, 1, 1, 1, 0},
  {0, 0, 1, 0, 1, 0, 0, 0, 1, 0, 0, 0, 0, 1, 0},
  {0, 1, 1, 1, 1, 1, 1, 1, 1, 1, 1, 1, 0, 1, 0},
  {0, 0, 0, 0, 0, 0, 0, 0, 0, 0, 0, 0, 0, 1, 0}
};
```

Listing 10-1: MazeSolver.cpp

The entrance of the maze is at the top left corner, and the exit at the bottom right corner.

We will use a stack structure to solve this maze. As we move through the maze, we store the entered point coordinates in the stack. When we reach a dead end, then we will have to backtrack, and we will do this by popping one point from the stack. This algorithm is called *Depth-first search (DFS)*, as it goes inside the maze as deep as possible, only to go back and try another direction when no way is found.

Here is the code for the coordinate points:

```
#include <iostream>
#define ROWS 15
#define COLS 15
using namespace std;

class Point
{
public:
  int row, col;

  Point()
  {
    row = 0;
```

```
      col = 0;
  }

  Point(int x, int y)
  {
    row = x;
    col = y;
  }
};
```

Listing 10-2: MazeSolver.cpp

And here is the code for the stack:

```
template <class T>
class Stack
{
  T* items;
  int top;

public:
  Stack(int capacity)
  {
    items = new T[capacity];
    top = -1;
  }

  bool is_empty()
  {
    return top == -1;
  }

  void push(T t)
  {
    top++;
    items[top] = t;
  }

  T pop()
  {
    return items[top--];
  }
};
```

Listing 10-2: MazeSolver.cpp

To make it more interesting, we have created a stack using C++ class templates. The stack will eventually contain an array of point coordinates. We have defined functions to initialize the stack, to check if it's empty, as well as to push and pop objects in the stack.

Now, it is time to introduce a class that will handle the maze:

```
class Maze
{
  Stack<Point> stack;

  int matrix[ROWS][COLS] = {
    {0, 1, 0, 0, 0, 0, 0, 0, 0, 0, 0, 0, 0, 0, 0},
    {0, 1, 0, 1, 0, 1, 1, 1, 1, 0, 1, 1, 1, 1, 0},
    {0, 1, 0, 1, 0, 1, 0, 0, 0, 0, 1, 0, 0, 0, 0},
    {0, 0, 0, 1, 0, 1, 0, 1, 1, 1, 1, 0, 1, 1, 0},
    {0, 1, 0, 1, 0, 1, 0, 0, 0, 0, 1, 0, 1, 0, 0},
    {0, 1, 0, 1, 0, 1, 1, 1, 1, 0, 1, 0, 1, 1, 0},
    {0, 1, 0, 1, 0, 0, 0, 0, 1, 0, 1, 0, 0, 0, 0},
    {0, 1, 0, 1, 1, 1, 1, 0, 1, 0, 1, 0, 1, 1, 0},
    {0, 1, 0, 0, 0, 0, 1, 0, 1, 0, 1, 0, 0, 1, 0},
    {0, 1, 1, 1, 1, 0, 1, 0, 1, 0, 1, 0, 1, 1, 0},
    {0, 0, 0, 0, 1, 0, 1, 0, 1, 0, 1, 0, 0, 0, 0},
    {0, 1, 1, 0, 1, 0, 1, 0, 1, 0, 1, 1, 1, 1, 0},
    {0, 0, 1, 0, 1, 0, 0, 0, 1, 0, 0, 0, 0, 1, 0},
    {0, 1, 1, 1, 1, 1, 1, 1, 1, 1, 1, 1, 0, 1, 0},
    {0, 0, 0, 0, 0, 0, 0, 0, 0, 0, 0, 0, 0, 1, 0}
  };

public:
  Maze();
  bool canMove(int row, int col);
  void print();
  void print_path();
  int solve(int row, int col);
};
```
Listing 10-4: MazeSolver.cpp

The class constructor initializes the stack with a capacity for 15*15 items:

```
Maze::Maze() : stack(ROWS* COLS) { }
```

Listing 10-5: MazeSolver.cpp

Next, we add the code to check whether we can move to a cell:

```
// Check if we can move to this cell
bool Maze::canMove(int row, int col)
{
  return (row >= 0
            && row < ROWS
            && col >= 0
            && col < COLS
            && matrix[row][col] == 0);
}
```

Listing 10-6: MazeSolver.cpp

The cell must me within the maze bounds and should be part of a corridor.

We also provide a function to print the maze:

```cpp
void Maze::print()
{
  for (int i = 0; i < ROWS; i++) {
    for (int j = 0; j < COLS; j++)
    {
      cout << matrix[i][j] << " ";
    }
    cout << "" << endl;
  }
}
```

Listing 10-7: MazeSolver.cpp

The following function implements the maze solving algorithm:

```cpp
// Solve the maze using backtracking
int Maze::solve(int row, int col)
{
  if (row == ROWS - 1 && col == COLS - 1)
  {
    // destination reached
    stack.push(Point(row, col));
    return 1;
  }

  if (canMove(row, col))
  {
    stack.push(Point(row, col));
    matrix[row][col] = 2; // Marking visited

    // Move right
    if (solve(row, col + 1))
      return 1;

    // Move down
    if (solve(row + 1, col))
      return 1;

    // Move left
    if (solve(row, col - 1))
      return 1;

    // Move up
    if (solve(row - 1, col))
      return 1;

    // If none of the above movements work, backtrack
    stack.pop();
    return 0;
  }

  return 0;
}
```

Listing 10-8: MazeSolver.cpp

First of all, we check whether the destination has been reached, by comparing the current row and column with the constant values ROW and COL.

In the opposite case, we first check if we can actually move to this cell, i.e., if it is part of a corridor and is within the maze bounds. If so, we add its coordinates into the stack and we mark the cell with the number 2, to mark the fact that we have already passed from this cell.

Then, we proceed with calling recursively the solve() function for all four directions, starting with right and down, and then trying with left and up. If none of those movements results in solving the maze (i.e. they all return 0), then we will have to backtrack. Since this point in the maze was not eventually part of the solution, we pop it from the stack.

We also define a function to print the path followed to solve the maze. We get it by popping the visited cells of the maze from the stack, one by one:

```cpp
void Maze::print_path()
{
  while (!stack.is_empty()) {
    Point p = stack.pop();
    cout << "(" << p.row << ", " << p.col << "), ";
  }
}
```

Listing 10-9: MazeSolver.cpp

Finally, let's see the main function of the program:

```cpp
int main()
{
  Maze maze;

  cout << "This is the maze:" << endl;
  maze.print();

  if (maze.solve(0, 0))
  {
    cout << "\n\n This is the path found:" << endl;
    maze.print_path();

    cout << "\n\nThis is the maze with all the points crossed:" << endl;
    maze.print();
  }
  else
  {
    cout << "No path found" << endl;
  }
  return 0;
}
```

Listing 10-10: MazeSolver.cpp

We first print the initial maze, then we solve the maze and we print the solution path. Then we display the map once more; all the points that we crossed during our search will be marked with '2'.

You can find this project in GitHub:

https://github.com/htset/cpp_exercises_dsa/tree/master/MazeSolver

11. File Indexer

For this exercise, we will create a program that will recursively index all the files in a specified folder. The information about the indexed files (filename and location in the disk) will be stored in a *Binary Search Tree (BST)* for faster searching.

Proposed Solution

For this project we will use the FileSystem library from Boost (https://www.boost.org/).

We should follow the instructions to install and build the libraries in our computer (https://www.boost.org/doc/libs/1_84_0/more/getting_started/windows.html).

Then, in Visual Studio, we have to add two entries into the Project Settings:

- C/C++ → General → Additional Include Directories: the Boost root directory (e.g., C:\boost_1_84_0\)
- Linker → General → Additional Library Directories: the lib directory (e.g., C:\boost_1_84_0\stage\lib)

The Binary Search Tree structure is a tree where each node has only two children, left and right. Here is the definition of the class:

```cpp
#include <iostream>
#include <string>
#include <boost/filesystem.hpp>

namespace fs = boost::filesystem;

class FileIndexer
{
private:
  struct Node
  {
    std::string fileName;
    std::string filePath;
    Node* left;
    Node* right;

    Node(const std::string& name, const std::string& path)
      : fileName(name), filePath(path), left(nullptr), right(nullptr) {}
  };

  Node* root;

  void insert_node(const std::string& fileName, const std::string& filePath);
  void index_directory_helper(const fs::path& dirPath);
  void delete_subtree(Node* root);
  void traverse(Node* root);
```

```
public:
  FileIndexer() : root(nullptr) {}
  void index_directory(const std::string& directoryPath);
  void print_files();
  std::string search_file_location(const std::string filename);
  ~FileIndexer();
};
```

Listing 11-1: FileIndexer.cpp

Each node of the tree contains two strings, the filename and the file location. It also contains pointers to the two children nodes.

Next, we define a function to insert a new node into the tree:

```
// Insert node to tree
void FileIndexer::insert_node(const std::string& fileName, const std::string&
filePath)
{
  // If the tree is empty, insert node here
  if (root == nullptr)
  {
    root = new Node(fileName, filePath);
    return;
  }

  // If not empty, then go down the tree
  Node* current = root;
  while (true)
  {
    if (fileName < current->fileName)
    {
      if (current->left == nullptr)
      {
        current->left = new Node(fileName, filePath);
        return;
      }
      current = current->left;
    }
    else
    {
      if (current->right == nullptr)
      {
        current->right = new Node(fileName, filePath);
        return;
      }
      current = current->right;
    }
  }
}
```

Listing 11-2: FileIndexer.cpp

Starting from the root of the tree, we move downwards to the left or to the right depending on the inserted value.

Next, we define the function that will recursively index all files into the tree:

```cpp
// Index the specified directory
void FileIndexer::index_directory_helper(const fs::path& dirPath)
{
  //if it's not a directory, return
  if (!fs::exists(dirPath) || !fs::is_directory(dirPath))
    return;

  //get iterator of files within directory
  for (const auto& entry : fs::directory_iterator(dirPath))
  {
    if (fs::is_regular_file(entry))
    {
      std::string fileName = entry.path().filename().string();
      std::string filePath = entry.path().string();
      insert_node(fileName, filePath);
    }
    else if (fs::is_directory(entry))
    {
      //recursively index sub-directory
      index_directory_helper(entry);
    }
  }
}
```

Listing 11-3: FileIndexer.cpp

We use the Boost FileSystem functions to check if a path exists (`fs::exists()`) and corresponds to a directory (`fs::is_directory()`). We then obtain an iterator that enables us to get all the files inside the directory, one by one.

If an entry is a regular file (`fs::is_regular_file()`), then we insert it in the tree as a new node.

If we stumble on a sub-directory (`fs::is_directory()`), we also index it recursively.

Next, we define a function to recursively delete the nodes of the tree:

```cpp
// Deallocate memory recursively
void FileIndexer::delete_subtree(Node* root)
{
  if (root != nullptr)
  {
    delete_subtree(root->left);
    delete_subtree(root->right);
    delete root;
  }
}
```

Listing 11-4: FileIndexer.cpp

Then, we have the directory traversal function (also recursive):

```cpp
void FileIndexer::traverse(Node* root)
{
  if (root != nullptr)
  {
    traverse(root->left);
    std::cout << root->fileName << ": " << root->filePath << std::endl;
    traverse(root->right);
  }
}
```

Listing 11-5: FileIndexer.cpp

Now, we turn to the *public* interface provided by the FileIndexer class. We define functions to index and print all the files in a directory. Those functions call the respective private helper functions:

```cpp
void FileIndexer::index_directory(const std::string& directoryPath)
{
  root = nullptr;
  index_directory_helper(directoryPath);
}

void FileIndexer::print_files()
{
  std::cout << "Indexed files:" << std::endl;
  traverse(root);
}
```

Listing 11-6: FileIndexer.cpp

After the tree has been set up, we can call function search_file_location() to get the location of a file:

```cpp
// Search for a file in the BST
std::string FileIndexer::search_file_location(const std::string filename)
{
  // Traverse the tree until a match is found or the tree is exhausted
  while (root != nullptr)
  {
    if (filename == root->fileName)
    {
      return root->filePath; // File found
    }
    else if (filename < root->fileName)
    {
      root = root->left; // Search in the left subtree
    }
    else
    {
      root = root->right; // Search in the right subtree
```

```
    }
  }
  return ""; // File not found
}
```

Listing 11-7: FileIndexer.cpp

We traverse the tree until we find a node with the specified file name. If the tree is exhausted, then we return null.

The class destructor proceeds to free memory allocated to the tree:

```
FileIndexer::~FileIndexer()
{
  // Call deleteSubtree to deallocate memory for the binary search tree nodes
  delete_subtree(root);
}
```

Listing 11-8: FileIndexer.cpp

Finally, here is the main() function:

```
int main()
{
  std::string path;
  std::cout << "Path to index recursively: ";
  std::getline(std::cin, path);

  FileIndexer indexer;
  indexer.index_directory(path);
  indexer.print_files();

  std::string filenameToSearch;
  std::cout << "Let's search for a file's location. Give the file name: ";
  std::getline(std::cin, filenameToSearch);

  std::string location = indexer.search_file_location(filenameToSearch);
  if (location != "")
  {
    std::cout << "File " << filenameToSearch << " found. Location: "
      << location << std::endl;
  }
  else
  {
    std::cout << "File " << filenameToSearch << " not found. " << std::endl;
  }
  return 0;
}
```

Listing 11-9: FileIndexer.cpp

Users can index the contents of a folder and then they can search for a specific filename.

You can find this project in GitHub:

https://github.com/htset/cpp_exercises_dsa/tree/master/FileIndexer

12. Inventory with AVL Tree

In this exercise, we will create an inventory program, that will store information about the company's products in an AVL tree structure.

Proposed Solution

An *AVL (Adelson-Velsky and Landis) tree* is a *self-balancing* binary search tree structure. With the term *balanced*, we mean that both branches of the tree have the same depth or differ by one level at the most. To achieve this, a process called *rebalancing* is occasionally performed, that changes the tree structure in way that the tree is closer to be balanced.

The AVL tree has almost the same structure as a simple binary search tree (BST); the difference lies in the rebalancing algorithm. Let's see the structure:

```cpp
#include <iostream>
#include <string>
#include <ctime>
using namespace std;

class Product
{
public:
    int id;
    string name;
    float price;
    int quantity;
};

class InventoryNode
{
public:
    Product product;
    InventoryNode* left;
    InventoryNode* right;
    int height;
};
```

Listing 12-1: InventoryAVL.cpp

The `InventoryNode` class contains a product object and two pointers to the tree's branches. Most importantly, it also contains the `height` property, which is used to track the tree's height.

Next, we define the `Inventory` class:

```cpp
class Inventory
{
private:
    InventoryNode *root;

    int get_height(InventoryNode* node);
```

```cpp
    int get_balance(InventoryNode* node);
    InventoryNode* new_node(Product product);
    InventoryNode* rotate_right(InventoryNode* y);
    InventoryNode* rotate_left(InventoryNode* x);
    InventoryNode* insert_product(InventoryNode* node, Product product);
    void traverse_tree(InventoryNode* node);
    InventoryNode* search_product(InventoryNode* node, int id);

public:
    Inventory() { root = nullptr; }
    void insert_product(Product product);
    void traverse_tree();
    InventoryNode* search_product(int id);
};
```

Listing 12-2: InventoryAVL.cpp

The Inventory class contains a pointer that is the root of the AVL tree.

Next, we define two internal functions of the tree:

```cpp
int Inventory::get_height(InventoryNode* node)
{
    if (node == nullptr)
        return 0;
    return node->height;
}

int Inventory::get_balance(InventoryNode* node)
{
    if (node == nullptr)
        return 0;
    return get_height(node->left) - get_height(node->right);
}
```

Listing 12-3: InventoryAVL.cpp

The former gives us the height of the tree, while the latter checks whether the tree is balanced or not.

Afterwards, we add code for the creation of a new node in the tree:

```cpp
InventoryNode* Inventory::new_node(Product product)
{
    InventoryNode* node = new InventoryNode;
    if (node != nullptr)
    {
        node->product = product;
        node->left = nullptr;
        node->right = nullptr;
        node->height = 1;
        return node;
    }
    else
```

```
{
    cout << "Error allocating memory. Exiting...";
    exit(1);
  }
}
```

Listing 12-4: InventoryAVL.cpp

Note that the height of the node is set to 1.

Next, we proceed with the definition of two functions for the rotation of the tree to the left or to the right:

```
InventoryNode* Inventory::rotate_right(InventoryNode* y)
{
    cout << "right rotate" << endl;
    InventoryNode* x = y->left;
    InventoryNode* T2 = x->right;

    x->right = y;
    y->left = T2;

    y->height = max(get_height(y->left), get_height(y->right)) + 1;
    x->height = max(get_height(x->left), get_height(x->right)) + 1;

    return x;
}

InventoryNode* Inventory::rotate_left(InventoryNode* x)
{
    cout << "left rotate" << endl;
    InventoryNode* y = x->right;
    InventoryNode* T2 = y->left;

    y->left = x;
    x->right = T2;

    x->height = max(get_height(x->left), get_height(x->right)) + 1;
    y->height = max(get_height(y->left), get_height(y->right)) + 1;

    return y;
}
```

Listing 12-5: InventoryAVL.cpp

Those two functions will be used when we will try to insert a new node into the tree:

```
InventoryNode* Inventory::insert_product(InventoryNode* node, Product product)
{
    if (node == nullptr)
        return new_node(product);

    if (product.id < node->product.id)
        node->left = insert_product(node->left, product);
```

```
  else if (product.id > node->product.id)
    node->right = insert_product(node->right, product);
  else
    return node;

  node->height = 1 + max(get_height(node->left), get_height(node->right));

  int balance = get_balance(node);

  if (balance > 1 && product.id < node->left->product.id)
    return rotate_right(node);

  if (balance < -1 && product.id > node->right->product.id)
    return rotate_left(node);

  if (balance > 1 && product.id > node->left->product.id)
  {
    node->left = rotate_left(node->left);
    return rotate_right(node);
  }

  if (balance < -1 && product.id < node->right->product.id)
  {
    node->right = rotate_right(node->right);
    return rotate_left(node);
  }

  return node;
}
```

Listing 12-6: InventoryAVL.cpp

Next, we present the functions to traverse the tree while printing its contents, as well as the code to search for a specific product in the tree:

```
void Inventory::traverse_tree(InventoryNode* node)
{
  if (node != nullptr)
  {
    traverse_tree(node->left);
    cout << "ID: " << node->product.id
      << ", Name: " << node->product.name
      << ", Price : " << node->product.price
      << ", Quantity :" << node->product.quantity << endl;
    traverse_tree(node->right);
  }
}

InventoryNode* Inventory::search_product(InventoryNode* node, int id)
{
  if (node == nullptr || node->product.id == id)
  {
    if (node == nullptr)
      cout << "Product not found.\n";
```

```
    else
      cout << "Found product: ID: " << node->product.id
        << ", Name: " << node->product.name
        << ", Price : " << node->product.price
        << ", Quantity :" << node->product.quantity << endl;

    return node;
  }

  cout << "Visited product ID: " << node->product.id << endl;

  if (id < node->product.id)
    return search_product(node->left, id);
  else
    return search_product(node->right, id);
}
```

Listing 12-7: InventoryAVL.cpp

Traversing the tree means visiting each node in the tree, and this is performed recursively, first for the left branch and then for the right branch.

Searching for a product in the tree works in similar fashion: we visit a node, and we check the product's ID. If it matches the search ID, then we print the product details and the function returns. Otherwise, we visit the left or the right branch of the tree recursively, depending on the search ID.

All the functions we defined so far are private. We also define three public functions that will call them:

```
void Inventory::insert_product(Product product)
{
  root = insert_product(root, product);
}

void Inventory::traverse_tree()
{
  traverse_tree(root);
}

InventoryNode* Inventory::search_product(int id)
{
  return search_product(root, id);
}
```

Listing 12-8: InventoryAVL.cpp

We use this convention because the respective private functions with the same name (insert_product, traverse_tree and search_product) are called recursively. In this way, we provide a clean interface to programmers that will use our code.

Finally, here is the main() function:

```cpp
int main()
{
    Inventory inv;
    Product products[100];

    // Adding 100 random products
    srand((unsigned int)time(nullptr));
    for (int i = 0; i < 100; i++)
    {
        products[i].id = i + 1;
        products[i].name = "Product " + to_string(products[i].id);
        products[i].price = (float)(rand() % 1000) / 10.0;
        products[i].quantity = rand() % 100 + 1;
    }

    // Shuffle the array of products
    srand((unsigned int)time(nullptr));
    for (int i = 99; i > 0; i--)
    {
        int j = rand() % (i + 1);
        Product temp = products[i];
        products[i] = products[j];
        products[j] = temp;
    }

    for (int i = 0; i < 100; i++)
    {
        inv.insert_product(products[i]);
    }

    // Print inventory
    cout << "Inventory:" << endl;
    inv.traverse_tree();

    // Search for a product
    int productIdToSearch = 35;
    InventoryNode* foundProduct = inv.search_product(productIdToSearch);
    if (foundProduct != nullptr)
    {
        cout << "Product found:" << endl;
        cout << "ID: " << foundProduct->product.id
             << ", Name: " << foundProduct->product.name
             << ", Price : " << foundProduct->product.price
             << ", Quantity :" << foundProduct->product.quantity << endl;
    }
    else
    {
        cout << "Product with ID " << productIdToSearch << " not found." << endl;
    }
    return 0;
}
```

Listing 12-9: InventoryAVL.cpp

We create 100 products with random quantities and prices and place them in an array. Then we shuffle the array in a random order. Afterwards, we insert the products into the AVL tree and we print its contents.

Finally, a search is performed for a specific product ID. During the search process we print the visited nodes to get an idea of how fast we will find the specific ID inside the AVL tree.

You can find this project in GitHub:

https://github.com/htset/cpp_exercises_dsa/tree/master/InventoryAVL

13. Social Network

A social network is essentially a *graph* of nodes that depicts the users of the network along with their connections to their friends. In this exercise, we will create such a graph and we will implement the functionality to recommend new friends according to a user's current connections.

Proposed Solution

There are various ways to implement the users' graph, for example using *sparse two-dimensional matrices*. Here we will construct the graph with the use of a *one-dimensional array* of users, where the connections are stored in a linked list:

```cpp
#include <iostream>
#define MAX_USERS 100
using namespace std;

struct FriendNode
{
  string name;
  FriendNode* next;
};

struct User
{
  string name;
  FriendNode* friends;
};
```

Listing 13-1: SocialNetwork.cpp

The User struct contains the name of the user as well as a linked list of the user's friends.

Next, we define a *queue* class that will be used by the friend recommendation algorithm:

```cpp
class Queue
{
  struct QueueNode
  {
    int user_index;
    QueueNode* next;
  };

  QueueNode* front;
  QueueNode* rear;

public:
  Queue();
  bool is_empty();
  void enqueue(int user_index);
  int dequeue();
};
```

```cpp
Queue::Queue()
{
  front = rear = nullptr;
}

bool Queue::is_empty()
{
  return (front == nullptr);
}

void Queue::enqueue(int user_index)
{
  QueueNode* newNode = new QueueNode;
  newNode->user_index = user_index;
  newNode->next = nullptr;

  if (is_empty())
  {
    front = rear = newNode;
  }
  else
  {
    rear->next = newNode;
    rear = newNode;
  }
}

int Queue::dequeue()
{
  if (is_empty())
  {
    cout << "Queue is empty!" << endl;
    return -1;
  }

  QueueNode* temp = front;
  int user_index = temp->user_index;
  front = front->next;

  if (front == nullptr)
  {
    rear = nullptr;
  }

  delete temp;
  return user_index;
}
```

Listing 13-2: SocialNetwork.cpp

The queue contains the indexes of the users, as they will appear inside the users' array (see below in the Graph class). We define the struct for the queue nodes, and functions to enqueue and dequeue user indexes inside the queue, as well as to check whether it is empty or not.

Now, let's see how we will insert users into the graph and how we will define the connections with their friends. We define the Graph class, that essentially contains an array of all the users of the social network:

```cpp
class Graph
{
  User users[MAX_USERS];
  int num_users;

public:
  Graph();
  void add_user(string name);
  void add_connection(int src, int dest);
  void recommend_friends(int user_index);
};

Graph::Graph()
{
  num_users = 0;
}
```

Listing 13-3: SocialNetwork.cpp

Next, we provide the functionality to add a new user to the graph:

```cpp
void Graph::add_user(string name)
{
  if (num_users >= MAX_USERS)
  {
    cout << "Max user limit reached!" << endl;
    return;
  }

  users[num_users].name = name;
  users[num_users].friends = nullptr;
  num_users++;
}
```

Listing 13-4: SocialNetwork.cpp

We use the following method to add a new connection to a user:

```cpp
void Graph::add_connection(int src, int dest)
{
  if (src < 0 || src >= num_users || dest < 0 || dest >= num_users)
  {
    cout << "Invalid user index!" << endl;
    return;
  }

  FriendNode* new_node_src = new FriendNode;
```

```
  new_node_src->name = users[dest].name;
  new_node_src->next = users[src].friends;
  users[src].friends = new_node_src;

  FriendNode* new_node_dest = new FriendNode;
  new_node_dest->name = users[src].name;
  new_node_dest->next = users[dest].friends;
  users[dest].friends = new_node_dest;
}
```

Listing 13-5: SocialNetwork.cpp

Note that when we add a new connection, we make it bi-directional. That is, we insert a friend node for each one of the connection's ends.

Next, we proceed to the more interesting stuff, the recommender function:

```
void Graph::recommend_friends(int user_index)
{
  cout << "Recommended friends for " << users[user_index].name << ":" << endl;

  Queue queue;
  int visited[MAX_USERS] = { 0 };

  visited[user_index] = 1;
  queue.enqueue(user_index);

  while (!queue.is_empty())
  {
    int current_user_index = queue.dequeue();
    FriendNode* current = users[current_user_index].friends;

    while (current != nullptr)
    {
      int friend_index = -1;
      for (int i = 0; i < num_users; i++)
      {
        if (current->name == users[i].name)
        {
          friend_index = i;
          break;
        }
      }

      if (friend_index != -1 && !visited[friend_index])
      {
        cout << "- " << current->name << endl;
        visited[friend_index] = 1;
        queue.enqueue(friend_index);
      }

      current = current->next;
    }
  }
}
```

}

Listing 13-6: SocialNetwork.cpp

As already mentioned, the algorithm makes use of a queue. In the queue, we store the indexes of the user's friends as we follow the linked list. We then use the queue to get the friends of the user's friends, and in this way, we are able to travel through the connection of the graph and find all the connected people to the specific user.

Note that we are using the visited[] array to store the persons that we have already visited. This will prevent the algorithm for looping to the same friends again and again and will ensure the convergence of our search.

Finally, here is the main() function:

```cpp
int main()
{
    Graph graph;
    graph.add_user("User A");
    graph.add_user("User B");
    graph.add_user("User C");
    graph.add_user("User D");
    graph.add_user("User E");
    graph.add_user("User F");
    graph.add_user("User G");
    graph.add_user("User H");

    graph.add_connection(0, 1);
    graph.add_connection(1, 2);
    graph.add_connection(2, 3);
    graph.add_connection(4, 5);
    graph.add_connection(5, 7);
    graph.add_connection(3, 6);

    graph.recommend_friends(0);
    graph.recommend_friends(1);
    graph.recommend_friends(7);

    return 0;
}
```

Listing 13-7: SocialNetwork.cpp

In main(), we add users to the graph and we enter their friend connections. Then we run the algorithm to get friend recommendations.

You can find this project in GitHub:

https://github.com/htset/cpp_exercises_dsa/tree/master/SocialNetwork

14. Flights

Let's create a console application that will maintain a list of flights between cities and that will find the best combination of flights in terms of ticket cost.

Proposed Solution

This problem involves creating a graph between the cities. This graph will be weighted, with the cost of the respective ticket. We will use *Dijkstra's algorithm* to find the cheapest path between two of those cities.

First, we define the `City` struct that will store a map of the connected cities and the respective costs:

```cpp
#include <iostream>
#include <vector>
#include <queue>
#include <unordered_map>
#include <unordered_set>
#include <stack>

using namespace std;

// Structure to represent each city
struct City
{
  string name;
  unordered_map<string, int> flights; // Map of connected cities and their costs
  City(string n) : name(n) {}
};
```

Listing 14-1: Flights.cpp

Next, we define the `FlightGraph` class:

```cpp
// Graph class to represent all cities and flights
class FlightGraph
{
public:
  void addCity(const string& name);
  void addFlight(const string& src, const string& dest, int cost);
  vector<string> findCheapestRoute(const string& src, const string& dest,
    int& totalPrice);
  void displayAllFlights(const string& src, const string& dest);
private:
  unordered_map<string, City*> cities; // Map of city names and their objects
  void dfs(const string& src, const string& dest, unordered_set<string>& visited,
    stack<string> path);
  void printPath(stack<string> path);
};
```

Listing 14-2: Flights.cpp

This class contains all the cities objects in a map along with their names. We can add cities and flights to our graph with the following functions:

```cpp
// Add a city to the graph
void FlightGraph::addCity(const string& name)
{
    cities[name] = new City(name);
}

// Add a flight between two cities and its cost
void FlightGraph::addFlight(const string& src, const string& dest, int cost)
{
    // Assuming flights are bidirectional
    cities[src]->flights[dest] = cost;
    cities[dest]->flights[src] = cost;
}
```

Listing 14-3: Flights.cpp

Note that we assume that flights are bidirectional, and that they have the same price in both directions.

Next, we calculate the cheapest route between two cities using Dijkstra's algorithm:

```cpp
// Function to find the cheapest route between two cities using Dijkstra's algorithm
vector<string> FlightGraph::findCheapestRoute(const string& src, const string& dest,
int& totalPrice)
{
    unordered_map<string, int> dist;
    unordered_map<string, string> prev;
    priority_queue<pair<int, string>, vector<pair<int, string>>, greater<pair<int,
string>>> pq;

    for (auto& city : cities)
    {
        dist[city.first] = INT_MAX;
        prev[city.first] = "";
    }

    dist[src] = 0;
    pq.push({ 0, src });

    while (!pq.empty())
    {
        string u = pq.top().second;
        pq.pop();

        for (auto& flight : cities[u]->flights)
        {
            string v = flight.first;
            int cost = flight.second;

            if (dist[u] != INT_MAX && dist[u] + cost < dist[v])
            {
```

```
            dist[v] = dist[u] + cost;
            prev[v] = u;
            pq.push({ dist[v], v });
        }
    }
}

// Reconstructing the path
vector<string> path;
string current = dest;
while (!prev[current].empty())
{
    path.push_back(current);
    current = prev[current];
}
path.push_back(src);
reverse(path.begin(), path.end());

// Calculate total price
totalPrice = dist[dest];

return path;
}
```

Listing 14-4: Flights.cpp

Initially, we initialize a dictionary to store the distances from the source city to every other city, marking the source city's distance as 0 and all other cities as infinity. We use a priority queue to process cities based on their distance from the source, dequeuing the city with the shortest distance first.

For each dequeued city, we examine its neighboring cities, updating their distances if a shorter path through the current city is found. This process continues until all cities are visited or until the destination city is reached.

Upon completion, we reconstruct the shortest path from the source to the destination using the information stored in the previous node map, facilitating the determination of the total price of the route.

To avoid getting stuck in loops during the graph traversal, we keep track of the cities visited in the current path (dist map). If a city has already been visited in the current path, we skip exploring flights from that city to prevent loops.

We can calculate and print all the possible flights between two cities using *Depth-First Search (DFS)*:

```
// Display all possible flights between two cities using DFS
void FlightGraph::displayAllFlights(const string& src, const string& dest)
{
    if (cities.find(src) == cities.end() || cities.find(dest) == cities.end())
    {
```

```
    cout << "Invalid cities entered." << endl;
    return;
  }

  unordered_set<string> visited;
  stack<string> path;
  path.push(src);
  dfs(src, dest, visited, path);
}
```

Listing 14-5: Flights.cpp

We see that function `displayAllFlights()` calls the recursive `dfs()` function:

```
// Recursive DFS function to find all flights between source and destination
void FlightGraph::dfs(const string& src, const string& dest,
  unordered_set<string>& visited, stack<string> path)
{
  visited.insert(src);

  if (src == dest)
  {
    printPath(path);
  }
  else
  {
    for (const auto& flight : cities[src]->flights)
    {
      if (visited.find(flight.first) == visited.end())
      {
        path.push(flight.first);
        dfs(flight.first, dest, visited, path);
        path.pop();
      }
    }
  }

  visited.erase(src);
}
```

Listing 14-6: Flights.cpp

The `dfs()` method in the `FlightGraph` class implements *Depth-First Search (DFS)* recursively to find all possible flights between a source and a destination city within a flight network.

It begins by marking the current city as visited and checks if it matches the destination city. If the destination is reached, it prints the current path. Otherwise, it explores all neighboring cities not yet visited by recursively calling itself for each neighbor.

During exploration, it pushes the neighboring city onto the `path` stack and continues the search until all possible paths from the current city are explored or until the destination is reached.

Upon backtracking, it removes the current city from the `path` stack and marks it as unvisited, allowing exploration of alternative paths. This process is repeated until all cities in the network are explored.

We use this stack to print the final path in `printPath()` function:

```cpp
// Helper function to print a path (stack content)
void FlightGraph::printPath(stack<string> path)
{
  stack<string> temp;
  while (!path.empty())
  {
    temp.push(path.top());
    path.pop();
  }
  while (!temp.empty())
  {
    cout << temp.top();
    temp.pop();
    if (!temp.empty())
      cout << " -> ";
  }
  cout << endl;
}
```

Listing 14-7: Flights.cpp

Finally in `main()`, we add cities and flights to the graph and we ask the user to select a pair of cities to calculate the best (cheapest) combination of flights:

```cpp
nt main()
{
  FlightGraph graph;

  graph.addCity("London");
  graph.addCity("Paris");
  graph.addCity("Berlin");
  graph.addCity("Rome");
  graph.addCity("Madrid");
  graph.addCity("Amsterdam");

  graph.addFlight("London", "Paris", 100);
  graph.addFlight("London", "Berlin", 150);
  graph.addFlight("London", "Madrid", 200);
  graph.addFlight("Paris", "Berlin", 120);
  graph.addFlight("Paris", "Rome", 180);
  graph.addFlight("Berlin", "Rome", 220);
  graph.addFlight("Madrid", "Rome", 250);
  graph.addFlight("Madrid", "Amsterdam", 170);
  graph.addFlight("Amsterdam", "Berlin", 130);

  string departure, destination;
  cout << "Enter departure city: ";
  cin >> departure;
```

```cpp
    cout << "Enter destination city: ";
    cin >> destination;

    // Display all possible flights
    cout << "All possible flights between " << departure
        << " and " << destination << ":" << endl;
    graph.displayAllFlights(departure, destination);

    // Find the cheapest route and total price
    int totalPrice;
    vector<string> route = graph.findCheapestRoute(departure, destination, totalPrice);

    // Display the cheapest route and total price
    cout << "Cheapest Route: ";
    for (string city : route)
    {
        cout << city << " -> ";
    }
    cout << "Total Price: " << totalPrice << endl;

    return 0;
}
```

Listing 14-8: Flights.cpp

You can find this project in GitHub:

https://github.com/htset/cpp_exercises_dsa/tree/master/Flights

15. MNIST Image Comparison

In this exercise, we will play with handwriting images from the MNIST database.

Proposed Solution

The MNIST database (http://yann.lecun.com/exdb/mnist/) is a set of images depicting handwritten digits. The images are of 28x28 dimension and are typically used when studying pattern recognition and machine learning techniques.

Source: Wikipedia

We will download the following file and we will unzip it in our project's directory:

http://yann.lecun.com/exdb/mnist/train-images-idx3-ubyte.gz

We will also rename it as *input.dat*.

The first 15 bytes of this file, contain metadata about the images, i.e. the number of the images and their dimensions. Therefore, we will start reading from the 16th byte in steps of 28x28=784 bytes.

First, we define the `Image` class that will store the image data in an array of `unsigned chars`:

```
#include <iostream>
#include <fstream>
#include <cmath>
#include <vector>
```

```
#define IMAGE_SIZE 784     // Size of each image (28x28)
#define META_DATA_SIZE 15 // Size of meta data at the beginning of the file

using namespace std;

// Structure to represent an image
class Image
{
public:
  unsigned char* data;
  int id;

  Image(unsigned char* data, int id);
  void print();
  double euclideanDistance(Image* img);
};
```

Listing 15-1: MNISTImages.cpp

Note that we use the `unsigned char` type to store the bytes of the image. This type is commonly used when dealing with raw binary data or when you need to ensure that values are treated as non-negative.

Next, we implement the Image constructor and a print function:

```
Image::Image(unsigned char* data, int id)
{
  this->id = id;
  this->data = new unsigned char[IMAGE_SIZE];
  memcpy(this->data, data, IMAGE_SIZE);
}

void Image::print()
{
  for (int i = 0; i < IMAGE_SIZE; i++)
  {
    if (data[i] == 0)
      cout << " ";
    else
      cout << "*";
    if (i % 28 == 0)
      cout << endl;
  }
}
```

Listing 15-2: MNISTImages.cpp

We also implement the function that will calculate the *Euclidean distance* between two images, the current image (denoted by the `this` pointer) and another one passed as input:

```
// Calculate Euclidean distance between two images
double Image::euclideanDistance(Image* img)
{
  double distance = 0.0;
```

```
   for (int i = 0; i < IMAGE_SIZE; i++)
   {
      distance += sqrt(pow((this->data[i] - img->data[i]), 2));
   }
   return sqrt(distance);
}
```

We are essentially calculating the sum of the differences between the respective bytes of two images. If the images are similar in content, then the distance will be minimized. Conversely, the distance will be higher, for images that have significant differences.

Now, let's see the main() function:

```
int main()
{
   vector<Image*> images;
   ifstream ifs("input.dat", ios::binary);
   unsigned char pixels[IMAGE_SIZE] = { 0 };

   if (!ifs.is_open())
   {
      cout << "Error opening file." << endl;
      exit(EXIT_FAILURE);
   }

   // Skip the meta data at the beginning of the file
   ifs.seekg(META_DATA_SIZE, ios::beg);

   int count = 0;
   // Read data from the file and insert images into the vector
   while (ifs.read((char*)pixels, IMAGE_SIZE))
   {
      images.push_back(new Image(pixels, count++));
   }

   cout << "Total images: " << count << endl;

   ifs.close();

   // Example: Find the closest image to a randomly selected image
   // Seed the random number generator
   srand(time(nullptr));

   // Generate a random index within the range of the list length
   int randomIndex = rand() % count;
   cout << "Random index: " << randomIndex << endl;

   Image* randomImage = images.at(randomIndex);
   randomImage->print();

   Image* closestImage = nullptr;
   double minDistance = INFINITY;
```

```
  int index = 0, minIndex = 0;

  for (int i = 0; i < images.size(); i++)
  {
    double distance = randomImage->euclideanDistance(images.at(i));
    if (distance != 0 && distance < minDistance)
    {
      minDistance = distance;
      minIndex = i;
      closestImage = images.at(i);
    }
  }

  // Output the label of the closest image
  cout << endl << "Closest image (distance=" << minDistance
       << ", index = " << minIndex << ")" << endl;

  // Print closest image
  closestImage->print();

  return 0;
}
```

Listing 15-4: MNISTImages.cpp

We use a vector object from the *C++ Standard Template Library (STL)* to store the image pointers.

After we open the *input.dat* binary file, we skip the first 15 bytes with seekg(). Then, in a loop, we read one image at a time (784 bytes) with read() and we add the pointer to the respective Image object into the vector.

Afterwards, we get a randomly selected image from the vector, and we print it using empty space where the byte is zero and an asterisk ('*') in places where the image bytes are non-zero. This way, we can get an idea of the handwriting digit that was chosen:

After printing the selected image, we iterate the vector, and we calculate the Euclidian distance between the randomly selected image and the currently selected image from the list. We maintain the minimum distance encountered and the corresponding image along with its ID.

At the end, we print the closest image that we got; it seems that the algorithm is working fine.

As a final note, this algorithm will take a lot of time to get the closest image, as it is checking all the images, one by one. There are other algorithms that will make this operation faster, albeit, with a loss of precision.

One such example is the Locality-Sensitive Hashing[2] (LSH) algorithm, a technique used for approximate nearest neighbor search in high-dimensional spaces. LSH is particularly useful when dealing with large datasets where traditional exact nearest neighbor search methods become computationally expensive.

You can find this project in GitHub:

https://github.com/htset/cpp_exercises_dsa/tree/master/MNISTImages

---

[2] https://en.wikipedia.org/wiki/Locality-sensitive_hashing

16. HTTP Server with Caching

In this exercise, we will create a simple HTTP server that will serve static content (only HTML files). The web server will make use of a cache mechanism that will keep the most recently served content, in order to boost the server's performance.

Proposed Solution (Windows)

The web server cache is a structure that stores the content that was previously sent to the client browser. The cache has limited space, so when it is filled up, we will need to empty the *least recently used (LRU)* entry in order to make space for the new entry. Moreover, when an entry is used by the server to send content to the client, then this entry is moved to the head of the list, as it is the more recently used entry.

Let's see the cache definition:

```
#include <iostream>
#include <fstream>
#include <sstream>
#include <string>
#include <string.h>
#include <cstdlib>
#include <winsock2.h>
#include <ws2tcpip.h>

#define PORT 8080
#define MAX_REQUEST_SIZE 1024
#define CACHE_SIZE 3

#pragma comment(lib, "ws2_32.lib")

using namespace std;

// Node structure for doubly linked list
class Node
{
public:
   string url;
   string content;
   Node* prev;
   Node* next;
};

// Cache structure
class LRUCache
{
   int capacity;
   int size;
   Node* head;
   Node* tail;

public:
```

```
  LRUCache();
  ~LRUCache();
  Node* createNode(string url, string content);
  void deleteNode(Node* node);
  void insertAtHead(Node* node);
  void moveToHead(Node* node);
  string getContent(string url);
  void putContent(string url, string content);
};

class HttpServer
{
  LRUCache cache;
public:
  HttpServer():cache() { }
  void handleRequest(SOCKET clientSocket);
};
```

Listing 16-1: WebServerCache.cpp

The cache is implemented as a *doubly linked list*. In this kind of linked list, we can move to both directions, forward and backward. The doubly linked list is beneficial in our case as we can efficiently remove and insert nodes anywhere in the list without needing to traverse the list from the beginning. The same effect could be achieved with simple linked lists, or even arrays, but with lower performance.

In the above listing, we also define the HttpServer class, that will provide the functionality to handle the HTTP requests to our web server.

Also, note this line:

```
#pragma comment(lib, "ws2_32.lib")
```

It instructs the linker to add the ws2_32.lib library to the list of library dependencies. This is alternative to adding it in the project properties at *Linker->Input->Additional dependencies*.

Next, we have the main() function of our program:

```
int main()
{
  HttpServer httpServer;
  WSADATA wsaData;
  SOCKET listenSocket, clientSocket;
  struct sockaddr_in serverAddr, clientAddr;
  int addrLen = sizeof(struct sockaddr_in);

  // Initialize Winsock
  if (WSAStartup(MAKEWORD(2, 2), &wsaData) != 0)
  {
    perror("WSAStartup");
```

```cpp
        return 1;
    }

    // Create socket
    if ((listenSocket = socket(AF_INET, SOCK_STREAM, 0)) == INVALID_SOCKET)
    {
        perror("socket");
        return 1;
    }

    // Initialize server address
    memset(&serverAddr, 0, sizeof(serverAddr));
    serverAddr.sin_family = AF_INET;
    serverAddr.sin_addr.s_addr = INADDR_ANY;
    serverAddr.sin_port = htons(PORT);

    // Bind socket to address
    if (bind(listenSocket, (struct sockaddr*)&serverAddr, sizeof(serverAddr)) ==
SOCKET_ERROR)
    {
        perror("bind");
        closesocket(listenSocket);
        WSACleanup();
        return 1;
    }

    // Listen for connections
    if (listen(listenSocket, SOMAXCONN) == SOCKET_ERROR)
    {
        perror("listen");
        closesocket(listenSocket);
        WSACleanup();
        return 1;
    }

    cout << "Server started on port " << PORT << endl;

    while (1)
    {
        // Accept connections
        if ((clientSocket = accept(listenSocket, (struct sockaddr*)&clientAddr,
&addrLen)) == INVALID_SOCKET)
        {
            perror("accept");
            continue;
        }

        char* str = new char[INET_ADDRSTRLEN];
        inet_ntop(AF_INET, &(clientAddr.sin_addr), str, INET_ADDRSTRLEN);
        cout << "Connection from " << str << endl;
        // Handle client request
        httpServer.handleRequest(clientSocket);

        // Close client socket
```

```cpp
    closesocket(clientSocket);
  }

  // Close server socket
  closesocket(listenSocket);

  // Cleanup Winsock
  WSACleanup();

  return 0;
}
```

Listing 16-2: WebServerCache.cpp

Here we create a server socket that continuously accepts HTTP connections from web browsers at port 8080. When a connection is accepted, then the handleRequest() function (from HttpServer) is called:

```cpp
// Handle HTTP GET requests
void HttpServer::handleRequest(SOCKET clientSocket)
{
  char request[MAX_REQUEST_SIZE];
  int bytesReceived = recv(clientSocket, request, sizeof(request), 0);
  if (bytesReceived <= 0)
  {
    perror("recv");
    return;
  }

  //create a string object
  string req = string(request);
  string url;
  char delimiter = ' ';
  //use istringstream to parse the string
  istringstream iss(req);

  //get the text until the delimiter (' ')
  getline(iss, url, delimiter);
  if(url != "GET")
  {
    perror("Only GET requests are supported.");
    return;
  }

  //get the next text until the delimiter (' ')
  getline(iss, url, delimiter);
  if (url == " ")
  {
    perror("Invalid request format.");
    return;
  }

  //locate content in cache
  string content = cache.getContent(url);
```

```cpp
if (content == "") //not found
{
  // Serve the page from disk
  ifstream file(url.substr(1, url.length()));
  if (!file.is_open())
  {
    // File not found, return 404 response
    char response[] = "HTTP/1.1 404 Not Found\n\n";
    cout << "File not found: " << url.substr(1, url.length()) << endl;
    send(clientSocket, response, strlen(response), 0);
    return;
  }

  string response;
  response = "HTTP/1.1 200 OK\nContent-Type: text/html\n\n";
  send(clientSocket, response.c_str(), strlen(response.c_str()), 0);

  char buffer[MAX_REQUEST_SIZE] = {0};

  while (file.read(buffer, sizeof(buffer)))
  {
    send(clientSocket, buffer, file.gcount(), 0);
  }
  //get the last bytes of the request, that are less than the buffer size
  send(clientSocket, buffer, file.gcount(), 0);
  file.close();
  cout << "Got content from file: " << buffer << endl;

  // Cache the page content
  cache.putContent(url, buffer);
}
else
{
  // Serve the page from cache
  string response;
  response = "HTTP/1.1 200 OK\nContent-Type: text/html\n\n";
  send(clientSocket, response.c_str(), strlen(response.c_str()), 0);

  send(clientSocket, content.c_str(), strlen(content.c_str()), 0);
}
}
```

Listing 16-3: WebServerCache.cpp

Initially, the web request is received into the `request` buffer. Then we use an `istringstream` object to parse the request and retrieve the request type and the URL; only GET requests are handled by our server.

We then use the request URL to search in the cache for a previously stored response for this URL. If such an entry is not found in the cache, then we open the requested HTML file (The HTML files are stored in the same folder as our executable), and we transmit its HTML content in the response. Note that, before sending the content, we must send the header of the response:

```
HTTP/1.1 200 OK\nContent-Type: text/html
```

If the URL is found in the cache, then we get the content from there and we send it with the response.

Let's see how we do this, in function getContent():

```cpp
// Get the content associated with a URL from the cache
string LRUCache::getContent(string url)
{
  Node* current = head;
  while (current != nullptr)
  {
    if (current->url == url)
    {
      moveToHead(current);
      cout << "Got content from cache: " << current->content << endl;

      return current->content;
    }
    current = current->next;
  }
  // Return empty string if the URL is not found in cache
  return "";
}
```

Listing 16-4: WebServerCache.cpp

We start from the head of the list, and we search for the URL in the cache's nodes. If we find the URL, then we move the node to the head of the cache (the *most recently used entry*) and we return the stored HTML content. The function returns NULL if the URL is not found in the cache.

When a page is read from its file, then we store its content into the cache, with putContent():

```cpp
// Put a URL-content pair into the cache
void LRUCache::putContent(string url, string content)
{
  if (size == CACHE_SIZE)
  {
    deleteNode(tail);
    size--;
  }
  Node* newNode = createNode(url, content);
  insertAtHead(newNode);
  size++;
}
```

Listing 16-5: WebServerCache.cpp

If we have reached the maximum cache size, then the *LRU algorithm* kicks in: we delete the least recently used entry (the node at the tail of the list) and we make space for the insertion of the new entry (at the head of the list).

Now we can examine the functions that handle the cache operations. First, let's see how we can create a new node:

```
// Create a new node
Node* LRUCache::createNode(string url, string content)
{
  Node* newNode = new Node;
  newNode->url = url;
  newNode->content = content;
  newNode->prev = nullptr;
  newNode->next = nullptr;
  cout << "New node created: " << content << endl;
  return newNode;
}
```

Listing 16-6: WebServerCache.cpp

Next, we see how to insert a new node at the head of the cache:

```
// Insert a new node at the head of the cache
void LRUCache::insertAtHead(Node* node)
{
  node->next = head;
  node->prev = nullptr;
  if (head != nullptr)
  {
    head->prev = node;
  }
  head = node;
  if (tail == nullptr)
  {
    tail = node;
  }
  cout << "Node inserted at head: " << node->content << endl;
}
```

Listing 16-7: WebServerCache.cpp

Note that in all operations we have to take care of all four pointers: head, tail, next, prev.

As part of the LRU algorithm, we have to move a node to the head of the list:

```
// Move a node to the head of the cache
void LRUCache::moveToHead(Node* node)
{
  if (node == head)
  {
    // Node is already at the head, no need to move
```

```
    return;
  }

  // Adjust pointers to remove node from its current position
  if (node->prev != nullptr)
  {
    node->prev->next = node->next;
  }
  if (node->next != nullptr)
  {
    node->next->prev = node->prev;
  }

  // Update pointers to insert node at the head
  node->prev = nullptr;
  node->next = head;
  if (head != nullptr)
  {
    head->prev = node;
  }
  head = node;
  if (tail == nullptr)
  {
    tail = node;
  }
  cout << "Node moved to head: " << node->content << endl;
}
```

Listing 16-8: WebServerCache.cpp

Finally, here is the code for node deletion:

```
// Delete a node from the cache
void LRUCache::deleteNode(Node* node)
{
  if (node == nullptr)
    return;

  // If the node is the head of the list
  if (node == head)
  {
    head = node->next;
  }

  // If the node is the tail of the list
  if (node == tail)
  {
    tail = node->prev;
  }

  // Adjust pointers of neighboring nodes
  if (node->prev != nullptr)
  {
    node->prev->next = node->next;
  }
```

```
if (node->next != nullptr)
{
   node->next->prev = node->prev;
}
cout << "Node deleted: " << node->content << endl;

delete node;
}
```

We make sure to release the memory that was used for this node, in order to avoid memory leaks.

Finaly, here is the constructor and the destructor of the LRUCache class:

```
LRUCache::LRUCache()
{
   capacity = CACHE_SIZE;
   size = 0;
   head = nullptr;
   tail = nullptr;
}

LRUCache::~LRUCache()
{
   // Free cache memory
   Node* current = head;
   while (current != nullptr)
   {
      Node* temp = current;
      current = current->next;
      deleteNode(temp);
   }
}
```

In the destructor, we delete the nodes of the linked list one-by-one, freeing the allocated memory.

Proposed Solution (Linux)

Here is the same code for Linux:

```
#include <iostream>
#include <fstream>
#include <sstream>
#include <string>
#include <string.h>
#include <sys/socket.h>
#include <netinet/in.h>
```

```cpp
#include <arpa/inet.h>
#include <unistd.h>
#include <errno.h>

#define PORT 8080
#define MAX_REQUEST_SIZE 1024
#define CACHE_SIZE 3

using namespace std;

// Node structure for doubly linked list
class Node
{
public:
  string url;
  string content;
  Node *prev;
  Node *next;
};

// Cache structure
class LRUCache
{
  int capacity;
  int size;
  Node *head;
  Node *tail;

public:
  LRUCache();
  ~LRUCache();
  Node *createNode(string url, string content);
  void deleteNode(Node *node);
  void insertAtHead(Node *node);
  void moveToHead(Node *node);
  string getContent(string url);
  void putContent(string url, string content);
};

class HttpServer
{
  LRUCache cache;

public:
  HttpServer() : cache() {}
  void handleRequest(int clientSocket);
};

int main()
{
  HttpServer httpServer;
  int serverSocket, clientSocket;
  struct sockaddr_in serverAddr, clientAddr;
  socklen_t addrSize;
```

```cpp
// Create socket
serverSocket = socket(AF_INET, SOCK_STREAM, 0);
if (serverSocket < 0)
{
  perror("Socket creation failed");
  return errno;
}

// Bind socket
serverAddr.sin_family = AF_INET;
serverAddr.sin_addr.s_addr = INADDR_ANY;
serverAddr.sin_port = htons(PORT);
if (bind(serverSocket, (struct sockaddr *)&serverAddr, sizeof(serverAddr)) < 0)
{
  perror("Socket binding failed");
  return errno;
}

// Listen for connections
if (listen(serverSocket, 5) < 0)
{
  perror("Listen failed");
  return errno;
}

cout << "Server listening on port " << PORT << endl;

while (1)
{
  addrSize = sizeof(clientAddr);
  // Accept incoming connection
  clientSocket = accept(serverSocket, (struct sockaddr *)&clientAddr, &addrSize);
  if (clientSocket < 0)
  {
    perror("Accept failed");
    return errno;
  }

  // Convert client IP address and port to printable format
  char clientIP[INET_ADDRSTRLEN];
  inet_ntop(AF_INET, &(clientAddr.sin_addr), clientIP, INET_ADDRSTRLEN);

  // Print connection information
  printf("Connection accepted from %s:%d\n", clientIP, ntohs(clientAddr.sin_port));

  // Handle client request
  httpServer.handleRequest(clientSocket);

  // Close client socket
  close(clientSocket);
}

// Close server socket
```

```cpp
    close(serverSocket);

    return 0;
}

/*****************
** HttpServer functions
*******************/

void HttpServer::handleRequest(int clientSocket)
{
    char request[MAX_REQUEST_SIZE];
    int bytesReceived = recv(clientSocket, request, sizeof(request), 0);
    if (bytesReceived <= 0)
    {
        perror("recv");
        return;
    }
    request[bytesReceived] = '\0';

    string req = string(request);
    string url;
    char delimiter = ' ';
    istringstream iss(req);

    getline(iss, url, delimiter);
    if (url != "GET")
    {
        perror("Only GET requests are supported.");
        return;
    }

    getline(iss, url, delimiter);
    if (url == " ")
    {
        perror("Invalid request format.");
        return;
    }

    string content = cache.getContent(url);
    if (content == "")
    {
        // Serve the page from disk
        ifstream file(url.substr(1, url.length()));
        if (!file.is_open())
        {
            // File not found, return 404 response
            char response[] = "HTTP/1.1 404 Not Found\n\n";
            cout << "File not found: " << url.substr(1, url.length()) << endl;
            send(clientSocket, response, strlen(response), 0);
            return;
        }

        string response;
```

```cpp
    response = "HTTP/1.1 200 OK\nContent-Type: text/html\n\n";
    send(clientSocket, response.c_str(), strlen(response.c_str()), 0);

    char buffer[MAX_REQUEST_SIZE] = {0};

    while (file.read(buffer, sizeof(buffer)))
    {
      send(clientSocket, buffer, file.gcount(), 0);
    }
    send(clientSocket, buffer, file.gcount(), 0);
    file.close();
    cout << "Got content from file: " << buffer << endl;

    // Cache the page content
    cache.putContent(url, buffer);
  }
  else
  {
    // Serve the page from cache
    string response;
    response = "HTTP/1.1 200 OK\nContent-Type: text/html\n\n";
    send(clientSocket, response.c_str(), strlen(response.c_str()), 0);

    send(clientSocket, content.c_str(), strlen(content.c_str()), 0);
  }
}

/****************
** Cache functions
******************/

// Get the content associated with a URL from the cache
string LRUCache::getContent(string url)
{
  Node *current = head;
  while (current != nullptr)
  {
    if (current->url == url)
    {
      moveToHead(current);
      cout << "Got content from cache: " << current->content << endl;

      return current->content;
    }
    current = current->next;
  }
  // Return empty string if the URL is not found in cache
  return "";
}

// Put a URL-content pair into the cache
void LRUCache::putContent(string url, string content)
{
  if (size == CACHE_SIZE)
```

```
  {
    deleteNode(tail);
    size--;
  }
  Node *newNode = createNode(url, content);
  insertAtHead(newNode);
  size++;
}

// Create a new node
Node *LRUCache::createNode(string url, string content)
{
  Node *newNode = new Node;
  newNode->url = url;
  newNode->content = content;
  newNode->prev = nullptr;
  newNode->next = nullptr;
  cout << "New node created: " << content << endl;
  return newNode;
}

// Insert a new node at the head of the cache
void LRUCache::insertAtHead(Node *node)
{
  node->next = head;
  node->prev = nullptr;
  if (head != nullptr)
  {
    head->prev = node;
  }
  head = node;
  if (tail == nullptr)
  {
    tail = node;
  }
  cout << "Node inserted at head: " << node->content << endl;
}

// Move a node to the head of the cache
void LRUCache::moveToHead(Node *node)
{
  if (node == head)
  {
    // Node is already at the head, no need to move
    return;
  }

  // Adjust pointers to remove node from its current position
  if (node->prev != nullptr)
  {
    node->prev->next = node->next;
  }
  if (node->next != nullptr)
  {
```

```cpp
    node->next->prev = node->prev;
  }

  // Update pointers to insert node at the head
  node->prev = nullptr;
  node->next = head;
  if (head != nullptr)
  {
    head->prev = node;
  }
  head = node;
  if (tail == nullptr)
  {
    tail = node;
  }
  cout << "Node moved to head: " << node->content << endl;
}

// Delete a node from the cache
void LRUCache::deleteNode(Node *node)
{
  if (node == nullptr)
    return;

  // If the node is the head of the list
  if (node == head)
  {
    head = node->next;
  }

  // If the node is the tail of the list
  if (node == tail)
  {
    tail = node->prev;
  }

  // Adjust pointers of neighboring nodes
  if (node->prev != nullptr)
  {
    node->prev->next = node->next;
  }
  if (node->next != nullptr)
  {
    node->next->prev = node->prev;
  }
  cout << "Node deleted: " << node->content << endl;

  delete node;
}

LRUCache::LRUCache()
{
  capacity = CACHE_SIZE;
  size = 0;
```

```
  head = nullptr;
  tail = nullptr;
}

LRUCache::~LRUCache()
{
  // Free cache memory
  Node *current = head;
  while (current != nullptr)
  {
    Node *temp = current;
    current = current->next;
    deleteNode(temp);
  }
}
```

Listing 16-11: WebServerCache.cpp

We have changed only the code inside the main() function so that we can use Linux sockets. A couple more adaptations have been made, outside main(); they are underlined in the code snippet above.

You can find this project in GitHub:

https://github.com/htset/cpp_exercises_dsa/tree/master/WebServerCache

https://github.com/htset/cpp_exercises_dsa/tree/master/WebServerCacheLinux

17. Distributed Auction

In this exercise, we will create a distributed auction, that will consist of an auction server that receives bids from multiple clients. The clients will communicate with the server via sockets. The server will wait for 20 seconds (using a timer) for a new bid, or else the auction is over and the maximum bid wins. The timer will be reset upon timely submission of new bid.

Proposed Solution (Windows)

Let's start wih the auction server. The server should be able to accommodate multiple clients. For this reason, each client will be served in a separate *thread*, that will be spawned when the server socket accepts a new connection:

```cpp
#include <iostream>
#include <string>
#include <winsock2.h>
#include <windows.h>
#include <process.h>

#pragma comment(lib, "ws2_32.lib")

#define PORT 8080
#define MAX_CLIENTS 5

using namespace std;

// Structure to hold client information
typedef struct
{
  SOCKET socket;
  struct sockaddr_in address;
  int addr_len;
  int id;
} Client;

// Global variables for bid information
Client clients[MAX_CLIENTS];
HANDLE timer;
SOCKET server_socket;
int best_bid = 0;
int winning_client = 0;

VOID CALLBACK TimerCompletionRoutine(PVOID lpParam, BOOLEAN TimerOrWaitFired);
unsigned __stdcall client_handler(void* data);
```

Listing 17-1: AuctionServer.cpp

Here we define the Client struct that stores information about the connected client. We also define global variables, as well as the signature of two callback functions that will be implemented below.

Next, we have the main() function:

```cpp
int main()
{
  WSADATA wsa;
  struct sockaddr_in server_addr;
  int addr_len = sizeof(server_addr);

  // Initialize Winsock
  if (WSAStartup(MAKEWORD(2, 2), &wsa) != 0)
  {
    cout << "WSAStartup failed.\n";
    return 1;
  }

  // Create server socket
  if ((server_socket = socket(AF_INET, SOCK_STREAM, 0)) == INVALID_SOCKET)
  {
    cout << "Socket creation failed.\n";
    return 1;
  }

  // Prepare the sockaddr_in struct
  server_addr.sin_family = AF_INET;
  server_addr.sin_addr.s_addr = INADDR_ANY;
  server_addr.sin_port = htons(PORT);

  // Bind server socket
  if (bind(server_socket, (struct sockaddr*)&server_addr, sizeof(server_addr)) ==
SOCKET_ERROR)
  {
    cout << "Bind failed with error: " << WSAGetLastError() << endl;
    return 1;
  }

  // Listen to server socket
  if (listen(server_socket, 5) == SOCKET_ERROR)
  {
    cout << "Listen failed with error: " << WSAGetLastError() << endl;
    return 1;
  }
  cout << "Server listening on port " << PORT << endl;

  // Create a waitable timer
  timer = CreateWaitableTimer(NULL, TRUE, NULL);
  LARGE_INTEGER dueTime;
  dueTime.QuadPart = -200000000LL; // 20 seconds
  SetWaitableTimer(timer, &dueTime, 0, (PTIMERAPCROUTINE)TimerCompletionRoutine,
NULL, 0);

  while (1)
  {
    // Accept incoming connections and handle each client
    SOCKET client_socket;
```

```cpp
    Client client;
    client.addr_len = sizeof(client.address);

    // Accept connection from client
    if ((client_socket = accept(server_socket,
      (struct sockaddr*)&client.address, &client.addr_len)) == INVALID_SOCKET)
    {
      cout << "Accept failed with error: " << WSAGetLastError() << endl;;
      continue;
    }

    // Add client to the clients array
    int c = 0;
    for (int i = 0; i < MAX_CLIENTS; i++)
    {
      if (clients[i].socket == 0)
      {
        clients[i].socket = client_socket;
        clients[i].address = client.address;
        clients[i].addr_len = client.addr_len;
        clients[i].id = i + 1;
        c = i;
        cout << "Client no." << i+1 << " connected." << endl;
        break;
      }
    }

    // Handle client in a separate thread
    _beginthreadex(NULL, 0, client_handler, &clients[c], 0, NULL);
  }
  return 0;
}
```

Listing 17-2: AuctionServer.cpp

After initializing the Winsock library, we open a new *server socket*, and we listen for new connections. When a new connection arrives, we store the client details in an array and we spawn a new thread with _beginthreadex().

As an argument to this function we pass the address of the client_handler() callback function, that will handle the communication with the specific client.

Note also, that we create a *WaitableTimer* object. We set its due time to 20 seconds and we supply as argument the address of the other callback function, TimerCompletionRoutine(). This function will be called back when the timer expires, in order to handle the auction expiration event.

Now, let's see the first of the callback functions:

```cpp
// Callback function to handle client connection
unsigned __stdcall client_handler(void* data)
{
  Client* client = (Client*)data;
```

```cpp
    SOCKET client_socket = client->socket;
    char buffer[1024] = { 0 };
    int bid_amount;

    while (1)
    {
      // Receive bid amount from client
      int valread = recv(client_socket, buffer, sizeof(buffer), 0);
      if (valread <= 0)
      {
        if (valread == 0)
          cout << "Client disconnected. " << endl;
        else
          cout << "Recv failed with error: " << WSAGetLastError() << endl;

        break;
      }
      bid_amount = atoi(buffer);
      cout << "Received bid " << bid_amount << " from client " << client->id << endl;

      // Update best bid if necessary
      if (bid_amount > best_bid)
      {
        best_bid = bid_amount;
        winning_client = client->id;

        // Inform all clients about the new best bid
        string msg = "New best bid: " + to_string(best_bid) + "(Client: " +
to_string(winning_client) + ")";
        for (int i = 0; i < MAX_CLIENTS; i++)
        {
          if (clients[i].socket != 0)
          {
            send(clients[i].socket, msg.c_str(), strlen(msg.c_str()), 0);
          }
        }

        // Restart the timer
        LARGE_INTEGER dueTime;
        dueTime.QuadPart = -200000000LL; // 10 seconds in 100-nanosecond intervals
        SetWaitableTimer(timer, &dueTime, 0, (PTIMERAPCROUTINE)TimerCompletionRoutine,
NULL, 0);
      }
      else
      {
        string msg = "Received lower bid. Best bid remains at: " + to_string(best_bid);
        for (int i = 0; i < MAX_CLIENTS; i++)
        {
          if (clients[i].socket != 0)
          {
            send(clients[i].socket, msg.c_str(), strlen(msg.c_str()), 0);
          }
        }
      }
    }
```

```
    }
  return 0;
}
```

Listing 17-3: AuctionServer.cpp

Function `client_handler()` takes care of the communication with the client. This function gets as input a pointer to the `Client` struct, that was passed in `main()`:

```
_beginthreadex(NULL, 0, client_handler, &clients[c], 0, NULL);
```

Then, in an endless while loop, it blocks in the `resv()` function, waiting for input from the client. When a message arrives, the function is unblocked and continues to check the input. If the number of bytes read is 0, the client has disconnected. If it is equal to -1, then there was an error with the connection.

If the client has actually sent a valid bid, we compare it with the current maximum bid and we update this value if we got a higher bid. We also proceed with informing all clients about the submitted bid.

We also reset the timer to get a new 20 seconds' period. We achieve this by setting the timer again.

When the timer eventually expires, the `TimerCompletionRoutine()` function will be called:

```
// Callback function to finish the auction after 20 seconds of inactivity
VOID CALLBACK TimerCompletionRoutine(PVOID lpParam, BOOLEAN TimerOrWaitFired)
{
  cout << "Auction finished. Winning bid: " << best_bid << ", winner: client no." <<
winning_client << endl;

  // Inform all clients about the end of the auction
  string msg = "Auction finished. Winning bid: " + to_string(best_bid) + ", winner:
client no." + to_string(winning_client);
  for (int i = 0; i < MAX_CLIENTS; i++)
  {
    if (clients[i].socket != 0)
    {
      send(clients[i].socket, msg.c_str(), strlen(msg.c_str()), 0);
    }
  }

  CloseHandle(timer);
  closesocket(server_socket);
  WSACleanup();

  exit(EXIT_SUCCESS);
}
```

Listing 17-4: AuctionServer.cpp

After informing all clients about the winning bid, we close the timer handle and the server socket. After performing a cleanup of Winsock, we exit the program. The client sockets will be closed by the respective clients when they receive the message of the auction completion.

__stdcall is the calling convention used for the function. This tells the compiler the rules that apply for setting up the stack, pushing arguments and getting a return value.

Now for the auction client, we first implement the main() function:

```cpp
#include <iostream>
#include <stdlib.h>
#include <string>
#include <winsock2.h>
#include <Ws2tcpip.h>
#include <windows.h>
#include <process.h>

#pragma comment(lib, "ws2_32.lib")

#define PORT 8080
#define SERVER_IP "127.0.0.1"

using namespace std;

SOCKET client_socket;
int is_running = 1;
HANDLE receive_thread;

unsigned __stdcall receive_handler(void* arg);

int main()
{
  WSADATA wsa;
  struct sockaddr_in server_addr;
  int addr_len = sizeof(server_addr);

  // Initialize Winsock
  if (WSAStartup(MAKEWORD(2, 2), &wsa) != 0)
  {
    cout << "WSAStartup failed." << endl;
    return 1;
  }

  // Create socket
  if ((client_socket = socket(AF_INET, SOCK_STREAM, 0)) == INVALID_SOCKET)
  {
    cout << "Socket creation failed" << endl;
    return 1;
  }

  server_addr.sin_family = AF_INET;
  server_addr.sin_port = htons(PORT);
```

```cpp
    if (inet_pton(AF_INET, SERVER_IP, &server_addr.sin_addr) <= 0)
    {
      perror("inet_pton");
      closesocket(client_socket);
      WSACleanup();
      return 1;
    }

    if (connect(client_socket, (struct sockaddr*)&server_addr, sizeof(server_addr)) ==
SOCKET_ERROR)
    {
      cout << "Connect failed." << endl;
      closesocket(client_socket);
      WSACleanup();
      return 1;
    }

    cout << "Connected to server." << endl;

    receive_thread = (HANDLE)_beginthreadex(NULL, 0, receive_handler, NULL, 0, NULL);
    if (receive_thread == NULL)
    {
      perror("_beginthreadex");
      closesocket(client_socket);
      WSACleanup();
      return 1;
    }

    string buffer;
    while (is_running)
    {
      cout << "\nEnter your bid (or 'q' to quit): ";
      getline(cin, buffer);

      if (buffer == "q")
      {
        break;
      }

      if (send(client_socket, buffer.c_str(), strlen(buffer.c_str()), 0) ==
SOCKET_ERROR)
      {
        cout << "Send failed. " << endl;
        closesocket(client_socket);
        WSACleanup();
        return 1;
      }
    }

    return 0;
}
```

Listing 17-5: AuctionClient.cpp

Here, we create a client socket, and we connect to the server. If the connection is successful, we spawn a new thread that will be used to receive and print the information from the server.

The sending part of the communication, i.e. the submission of bids to the server, will be performed by the main thread. If we had the same thread handle sending and receiving of data, we would have a problem, as the recv() function would block and would not let the user send a new bid.

Here is the callback function for the thread handler:

```cpp
unsigned __stdcall receive_handler(void* arg)
{
  char buffer[1024] = { 0 };
  while (1)
  {
    int valread = recv(client_socket, buffer, sizeof(buffer), 0);
    if (valread <= 0)
    {
      if (valread == 0)
        cout << "\nServer disconnected." << endl;
      else
        perror("recv");

      break;
    }

    cout << "\nServer: " << buffer << endl;
    if (strncmp(buffer, "Auction", 7) == 0)
    {
      cout << "Auction ended. Exiting program." << endl;

      CloseHandle(receive_thread);
      closesocket(client_socket);
      WSACleanup();

      exit(EXIT_SUCCESS);
    }

    memset(buffer, 0, sizeof(buffer));
    cout << "\nEnter your bid (or 'q' to quit): ";
  }
  return 0;
}
```

Listing 17-6: AuctionClient.cpp

This thread receives messages from the auction server and prints them in console. When the final message, starting with "Auction" arrives, then it closes down the resources and exits the program.

Here is the code for the auction server:

```cpp
#include <iostream>
#include <stdlib.h>
#include <string.h>
#include <unistd.h>
#include <netinet/in.h>
#include <sys/socket.h>
#include <pthread.h>
#include <time.h>

#define PORT 8080
#define MAX_CLIENTS 5

using namespace std;

typedef struct
{
  int socket;
  struct sockaddr_in address;
  int addr_len;
  int id;
} Client;

Client clients[MAX_CLIENTS];
int server_socket;
int best_bid = 0;
int winning_client = 0;
pthread_mutex_t mutex = PTHREAD_MUTEX_INITIALIZER;
time_t last_bid_time;

void *timer_thread(void *arg);
void *client_handler(void *arg);

int main()
{
  struct sockaddr_in server_addr, client_addr;
  socklen_t client_addr_len = sizeof(client_addr);
  pthread_t threads[MAX_CLIENTS];
  pthread_t timer;
  time(&last_bid_time);

  // Create server socket
  if ((server_socket = socket(AF_INET, SOCK_STREAM, 0)) == -1)
  {
    perror("Socket creation failed");
    exit(EXIT_FAILURE);
  }

  // Bind server socket
  server_addr.sin_family = AF_INET;
```

```cpp
    server_addr.sin_addr.s_addr = INADDR_ANY;
    server_addr.sin_port = htons(PORT);
    if (bind(server_socket, (struct sockaddr *)&server_addr, sizeof(server_addr)) == -
1)
    {
      perror("Bind failed");
      close(server_socket);
      exit(EXIT_FAILURE);
    }

    // Listen for incoming connections
    if (listen(server_socket, MAX_CLIENTS) == -1)
    {
      perror("Listen failed");
      close(server_socket);
      exit(EXIT_FAILURE);
    }

    cout << "Server listening on port" << PORT << endl;

    // Create thread for timer
    if (pthread_create(&timer, NULL, timer_thread, NULL) != 0)
    {
      perror("Timer thread creation failed");
      close(server_socket);
      exit(EXIT_FAILURE);
    }

    while (1)
    {
      int client_socket;
      Client client;

      // Accept incoming connection
      client_socket = accept(server_socket, (struct sockaddr *)&client_addr,
&client_addr_len);
      if (client_socket == -1)
      {
        perror("Accept failed");
        close(server_socket);
        exit(EXIT_FAILURE);
      }

      // Add client to the clients array
      int c = 0;
      for (int i = 0; i < MAX_CLIENTS; i++)
      {
        if (clients[i].socket == 0)
        {
          clients[i].socket = client_socket;
          clients[i].address = client.address;
          clients[i].addr_len = client.addr_len;
          clients[i].id = i + 1;
          c = i;
```

```cpp
      cout << "Client no." << i+1 << " connected." << endl;
      break;
    }
  }

  if (pthread_create(&threads[c], NULL, client_handler, (void *)&clients[c]) != 0)
  {
    perror("Thread creation failed");
    close(server_socket);
    exit(EXIT_FAILURE);
  }
}

close(server_socket);

return 0;
}


void *client_handler(void *arg)
{
  Client *client = (Client *)arg;
  int client_socket = client->socket;
  char buffer[1024] = {0};
  int bid_amount;

  while (1)
  {
    // Receive bid from client
    ssize_t bytes_received = recv(client_socket, buffer, sizeof(buffer), 0);
    if (bytes_received == -1)
    {
      perror("Receive failed");
      break;
    }
    else if (bytes_received == 0)
    {
      cout << "Client disconnected." << endl;
      break;
    }

    pthread_mutex_lock(&mutex);
    bid_amount = atoi(buffer);
    cout << "Received bid " << bid_amount << " from client " << client->id << endl;
    if (bid_amount > best_bid)
    {
      best_bid = bid_amount;
      winning_client = client->id;

      // Inform all clients about the new best bid
      string msg = "New best bid: " + to_string(best_bid)
        + "(Client: " + to_string(winning_client) + ")";
      for (int i = 0; i < MAX_CLIENTS; i++)
      {
```

```cpp
        if (clients[i].socket != 0)
        {
          send(clients[i].socket, msg.c_str(), strlen(msg.c_str()), 0);
        }
      }
      time(&last_bid_time); // Update the last bid time
    }
    else
    {
      string msg = "Received lower bid. Best bid remains at: " + to_string(best_bid);
      for (int i = 0; i < MAX_CLIENTS; i++)
      {
        if (clients[i].socket != 0)
        {
          send(clients[i].socket, msg.c_str(), strlen(msg.c_str()), 0);
        }
      }
    }

    pthread_mutex_unlock(&mutex);
  }
}


void *timer_thread(void *arg)
{
  while (1)
  {
    time_t current_time;
    time(&current_time);
    double elapsed_seconds = difftime(current_time, last_bid_time);

    if (elapsed_seconds >= 20)
    {
      pthread_mutex_lock(&mutex);
      cout << "Auction finished. Winning bid: " << best_bid
        << ", winner: client no." << winning_client << endl;

      // Inform all clients about the end of the auction
      string msg = "Auction finished. Winning bid: " + to_string(best_bid)
        + ", winner: client no." + to_string(winning_client);
      for (int i = 0; i < MAX_CLIENTS; i++)
      {
        if (clients[i].socket != 0)
        {
          send(clients[i].socket, msg.c_str(), strlen(msg.c_str()), 0);
        }
      }
      close(server_socket);

      pthread_mutex_unlock(&mutex);

      exit(0);
    }
```

```
      sleep(1);
  }

  pthread_exit(NULL);
}
```

Listing 17-7: AuctionServer.cpp

Here we use the Unix socket functions, that are a bit different from Winsock. We also use the POSIX function pthread_create() to spawn a new thread.

The auction timer is implemented with sleeping for one second each time; After 20 seconds have elapsed without a new bid, the auction ends.

Here is the code for the auction client:

```
#include <iostream>
#include <stdlib.h>
#include <string.h>
#include <unistd.h>
#include <arpa/inet.h>
#include <netinet/in.h>
#include <sys/socket.h>
#include <pthread.h>

#define PORT 8080
#define SERVER_IP "127.0.0.1"

using namespace std;

int client_socket;

void *receive_handler(void *arg);

int main()
{
  struct sockaddr_in server_addr;
  pthread_t receive_thread;

  // Create client socket
  if ((client_socket = socket(AF_INET, SOCK_STREAM, 0)) == -1)
  {
    perror("Socket creation failed");
    exit(EXIT_FAILURE);
  }

  // Configure server address
  server_addr.sin_family = AF_INET;
  server_addr.sin_port = htons(PORT);
  if (inet_pton(AF_INET, SERVER_IP, &server_addr.sin_addr) <= 0)
  {
    perror("Invalid address");
    close(client_socket);
```

```cpp
        exit(EXIT_FAILURE);
    }

    // Connect to server
    if (connect(client_socket, (struct sockaddr *)&server_addr, sizeof(server_addr)) ==
-1)
    {
      perror("Connect failed");
      close(client_socket);
      exit(EXIT_FAILURE);
    }

    cout << "Connected to server." << endl;

    // Create thread to handle receiving messages from server
    if (pthread_create(&receive_thread, NULL, receive_handler, NULL) != 0)
    {
      perror("Thread creation failed");
      close(client_socket);
      exit(EXIT_FAILURE);
    }

    // Main thread to send messages to the server
    string buffer;
    while (1)
    {
      cout << "\nEnter your bid (or 'q' to quit): ";
      getline(cin, buffer);

      if (buffer == "q")
      {
        break;
      }

      if (send(client_socket, buffer.c_str(), strlen(buffer.c_str()), 0) == -1)
      {
        perror("Send failed");
        close(client_socket);
        exit(EXIT_FAILURE);
      }
    }

    return 0;
}

void *receive_handler(void *arg)
{
    char buffer[1024] = {0};

    while (1)
    {
      // Receive message from server
      ssize_t bytes_received = recv(client_socket, buffer, sizeof(buffer), 0);
      if (bytes_received == -1)
```

```cpp
    {
      perror("Receive failed");
      break;
    }
    else if (bytes_received == 0)
    {
      cout << "Server disconnected." << endl;
      break;
    }

    buffer[bytes_received] = '\0';
    cout << "\nServer: " << buffer << endl;

    if (strncmp(buffer, "Auction", 7) == 0)
    {
      cout << "Auction ended. Exiting program." << endl;

      close(client_socket);

      exit(0);
    }
    memset(buffer, 0, sizeof(buffer));
    cout << "\nEnter your bid (or 'q' to quit): ";
  }

  close(client_socket);
  pthread_exit(NULL);
}
```

Listing 17-8: AuctionClient.cpp

You can find this project in GitHub:

https://github.com/htset/cpp_exercises_dsa/tree/master/AuctionServer

https://github.com/htset/cpp_exercises_dsa/tree/master/AuctionClient

https://github.com/htset/cpp_exercises_dsa/tree/master/AuctionServerLinux

https://github.com/htset/cpp_exercises_dsa/tree/master/AuctionClientLinux